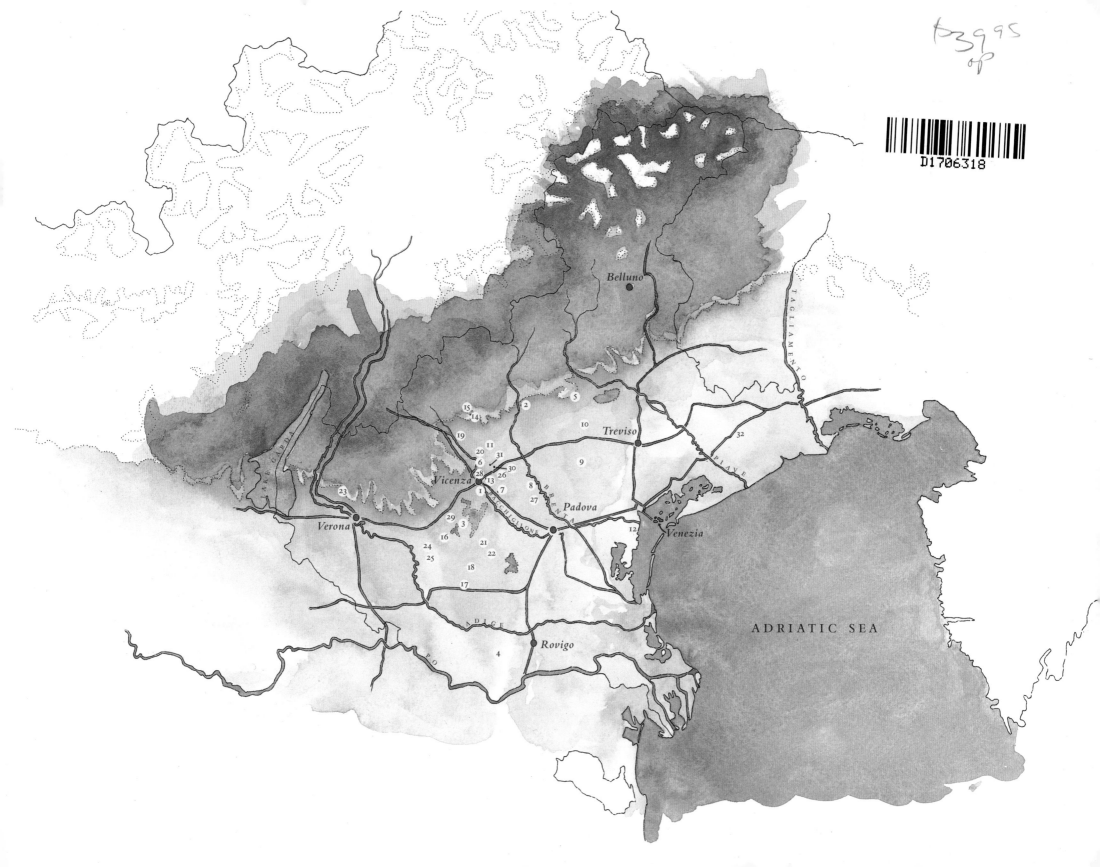

ADRIATIC SEA

Belluno

Treviso

Vicenza

Padova

Venezia

Verona

Rovigo

LAKE GARDA

TAGLIAMENTO

PIAVE

BRENTA

BACCHIGLIONE

ADIGE

PO

15
14
2
5
10
19
32
11
20
31
6
30
9
28
26
13
1
7
8
27
12
23
29
3
16
21
22
24
18
25
17
4

THE VILLAS OF PALLADIO

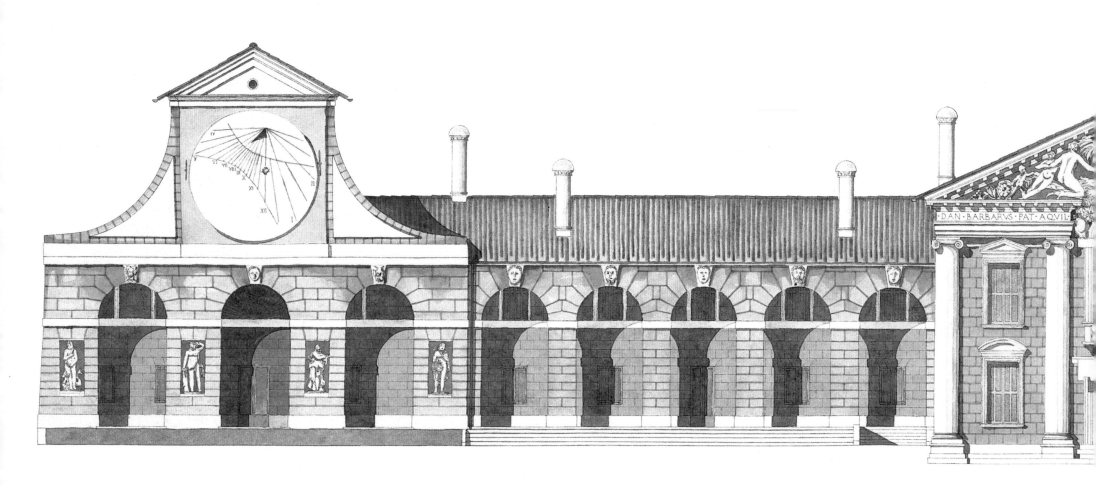

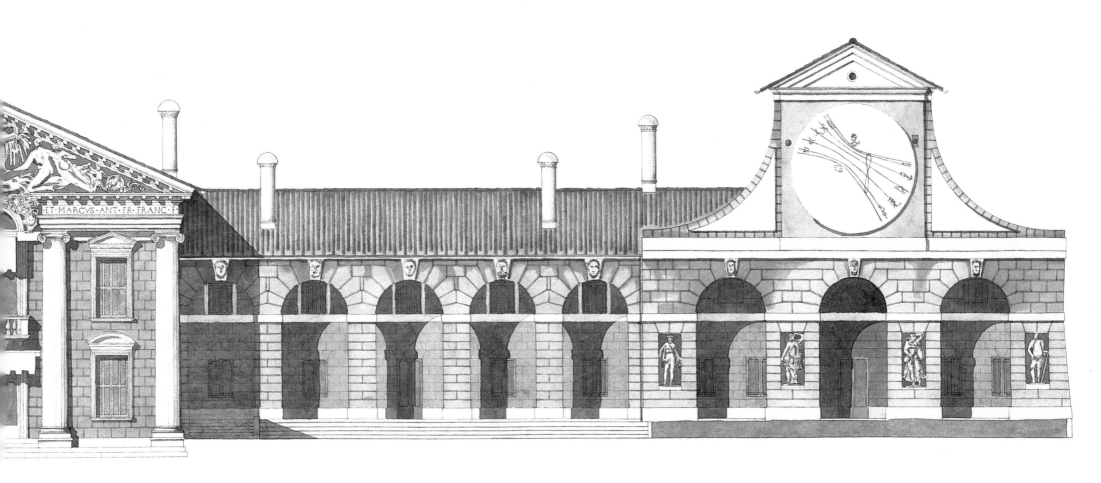

THE VILLAS

of

PALLADIO

Watercolors by
GIOVANNI GIACONI

Text by
KIM WILLIAMS

PRINCETON ARCHITECTURAL PRESS
NEW YORK 2003

Published by
Princeton Architectural Press
37 East Seventh Street
New York, New York 10003

For a free catalog of books, call 1.800.722.6657.
Visit our website at www.papress.com.

Visit Giovanni Giaconi's website at www.epalladio.com.

Editing: Nicola Bednarek
Design: Deb Wood

Special thanks to: Nettie Aljian, Ann Alter, Janet Behning, Megan Carey,
Penny (Yuen Pik) Chu, Russell Fernandez, Jan Haux, Clare Jacobson, Mark Lamster,
Nancy Eklund Later, Linda Lee, Nancy Levinson, Katharine Myers, Jane Sheinman,
Scott Tennent, Jennifer Thompson, and Joe Weston of Princeton Architectural Press
—Kevin C. Lippert, publisher

Library of Congress Cataloging-in-Publication Data
Williams, Kim.
  The villas of Palladio / watercolors by Giovanni Giaconi ; text by Kim
Williams.—1st ed.
     p. cm.
Includes bibliographical references.
  ISBN 1-56898-396-4
  1. Palladio, Andrea, 1508-1580. 2. Country homes—Italy, Northern.
3. Facades—Italy, Northern. 4. Giaconi, Giovanni. 5. Architectural
rendering—Italy. I. Giaconi, Giovanni. II. Palladio, Andrea,
1508-1580. III. Title.
  NA1123.P2 W55 2003
  728.8'092—dc21
                    2002154589

CONTENTS

ACKNOWLEDGMENTS
9
FOREWORD
11
INTRODUCTION
13
PLATES
21

22	Villa Trissino, *Cricoli*	84	Villa Badoer, *Fratta Polesine*
26	Villa Godi, *Lonedo*	88	Villa/barchessa Thiene, *Cicogna*
30	Villa Piovene, *Lonedo*	92	Villa Repeta, *Campiglia*
32	Villa Valmarana, *Vigardolo*	96	Villa Foscari, the "Malcontenta," *Malcontenta*
36	Villa Gazzotti, *Bertesina*	100	Villa Trissino, *Meledo*
40	Villa Pisani, *Bagnolo*	104	Villa Zeno, *Cessalto*
44	Villa Thiene, *Quinto Vicentino*	108	Villa Emo, *Fanzolo*
48	Villa Saraceno, *Finale*	112	Villa Valmarana, *Lisiera*
52	Villa Arnaldi, *Meledo Alto*	116	Villa Forni, *Montecchio Precalcino*
56	Villa Caldogno, *Caldogno*	120	Villa/barchessa Sarego, *Miega*
60	Villa Poiana, *Poiana Maggiore*	124	Villa Sarego, *Santa Sofia*
64	Villa Angarano, *Bassano del Grappa*	128	Villa Almerico, the "Rotonda," *Vicenza*
68	Villa Cornaro, *Piombino Dese*	132	Villa/barchessa Sarego, *Veronella*
72	Villa Pisani, *Montagnana*	134	Villa Porto, *Molina*
76	Villa Chiericati, *Vancimuglio*	138	Villa Contarini, *Piazzola sul Brenta*
80	Villa Barbaro, *Maser*	142	Villa Porto, *Vivaro*

NOTES
146

GLOSSARY
148

SELECTED BIBLIOGRAPHY
151

ACKNOWLEDGMENTS

Many people have helped to make this publication possible. I would like to offer my thanks to Richard Allon, Alessandro Basso, Francesca Romana Berno, Fabio Bischi, Marco Bordin, Joseph Cho, Marina Di Martino, Dario Galimberti, Giovanni Battista Gleria, Stefanie Lew, Conte Vettor Marcello, Ismaele Mason, Nello Olivieri, Gregory Piccininno, Luca Pizzaroni, Aldo Rapisarda, Bruno Riccone, and Sam Rohn, my supportive and encouraging friends.

The drawings and watercolors of Palladio's villas published in this book could not have been produced without the kind cooperation of the villas' owners. I am thankful to the Amministrazione Provinciale di Rovigo, Azienda Agricola Liasora, to Contessa Carla Bianchi Michiel, Emo Bressan, Margherita Bressan, Vigilio Bressan, Renato Bressan, Giovanni Brutto, Giandomenico Curti, Vittorio Dalle Ore, Contessa Carolyn Emo Capodilista, Contessa Cornelia Ferri de Lazara, the Fondazione G. E. Ghirardi, Antonio Foscari, Carl Gable, Sally Gable, Valerio Gasparetto, Lorella Graham, David Graham, The Landmark Trust (Shottesbrooke) UK, Diamante Luling Buschetti, Emma Malinverni, Christian Malinverni, Carlo Marcolin, the municipality of Quinto Vicentino, Marina Paparella, Massimo Pedrotti, Contessa Caterina Piovene Porto Godi, Giusto Placco, Pietro Rigo, Titta Rossi, Contessa Carolina di Serego, Laura Toson, Vittorio Trettenero, Alessandro Trettenero, Conte Lodovico Valmarana, Giovanni Zen, and the ownerships of Villa Arnaldi, Villa Forni, Villa Poiana, Villa Porto, and Villa Sarego in Santa Sofia.

I am grateful to Kim Williams for her insightful text accompanying the watercolors.

My very special thanks go to Mario Giaconi, Antonia Giaconi, Nicola Giaconi, Jolanda Giaconi, and Michele Giaconi, who have supported me in many ways.

GIOVANNI GIACONI

The mere mention of the villas of Palladio conjures up images of country life in Renaissance Italy: grand houses with columned porches set in commanding positions over fields and waterways. The villa has become a lasting part of the architectural vocabulary far beyond the time and geography of its genesis, and now belongs to all of the Western world. And although it was, as a distinct type of residential building, the product of a particular economic and social moment in the sixteenth century, Palladio's villas themselves outlived their creator and took on lives of their own, undergoing decay, reconstruction, destruction by fire, reconstruction, change of ownership, reconstruction. This present collection of meticulous watercolors by Giovanni Giaconi of the facades of thirty-two villas designed by Andrea Palladio presents a living record of the villas as they appear today, not as abstract ideals or as newborn conceptions, but as buildings with histories that can be read on their facades. The classic beauty of the villas' architectural designs and their evolution in time tell a story that goes well beyond the epoch in which they were designed, and is poignantly captured in these exquisite portraits.

Perhaps artist Giovanni Giaconi is so sensitive to Andrea Palladio's architecture because he, a Vicentine like Palladio, grew up with Palladio's architecture in Vicenza and the surrounding countryside. Like Palladio, Giaconi learned his trade by working rather than by academic study, honing his skills as a draftsman during an apprenticeship at architecture studios specializing in building conservation. Just as Palladio's villas are best understood in the context of a larger architectural and social tradition, Giaconi's watercolors of the villas must be seen not on their own, but in the context

of the tradition of architectural representations. Giaconi was drawn to the study of the villas of Palladio by his admiration for the drawings of Ottavio Bertotti-Scamozzi, who drew all of Palladio's buildings in the eighteenth century. Bertotti-Scamozzi's catalog of Palladio's architecture (*Le fabbriche e i disegni di Andrea Palladio*) is invaluable for gaining a sense of the architect's original aims and intentions, since many times the villas are represented not as they were at the time Bertotti-Scamozzi was recording them, but rather as he believed they were intended to be; a villa never actually completed might thus appear as it was designed rather than as executed. What Giaconi has chosen to do instead is to represent the villas exactly as they are, providing with this collection a living history of their evolution.

Giaconi's watercolors of the facades are as much an artistic creation as the architecture. The first step in their creation is a visit to the villa for several days of freehand sketching and measuring. Later, in his studio, Giaconi compiles the information he has gathered into a scale drawing in pencil on yellow tracing paper, incorporating at this stage the first studies of the play of light and shadow that produces the extraordinary depth of the finished watercolor. The next step is the drafting of a finished drawing of the facade in pen and ink on white tracing paper; Giaconi calls this drawing the "matrix," and it is the base for the final watercolor rendering. He photocopies the matrix onto watercolor paper, and then painstakingly applies the watercolors. The result is a faithful rendering of the facade of the villa as it is, or rather, as it was at the precise moment of the villa's representation. The villas are, of course, even today not static—indeed, now that we are on the eve of the five-hundredth anniversary of Palladio's birth they are the subject of quite a bit of attention. Villa Poiana, for instance, was carefully restored just a few years ago. Giaconi responded to this by returning to the villa and producing a new watercolor to reflect the restoration.

Giaconi's choice to represent the villas through a portrait of their facade rather than as an object in perspective reflects a particular tradition in the representation of architecture—a tradition that had a notable influence on Palladio's own draftsmanship as well as on his architecture. In the early sixteenth century, when Palladio was an apprentice, the forms and elements of the classical architecture of ancient Rome were studied through the copying of drawings by architects who had visited the sites. Palladio himself learned by copying the drawings of Raphael and Giulio Romano, among others. Some of Palladio's early sketches of buildings are in perspective, with lines projected toward one or more vanishing points, as opposed to an orthogonal depiction in which vertical elements and horizontal elements form true right angles, such as we see in the present collection of Giaconi. Since a drawing in perspective necessarily involves distortion, causing the true relationships between elements to be hidden, fifteenth-century architect and theorist Leon Battista Alberti, and later Raphael in the sixteenth century, drew a distinction between perspective depictions of architecture as pertaining to artists and orthogonal depictions as pertaining to architects. Acknowledging this distincion, Palladio later chose to redraw his earlier perspectives in the form of orthogonal elevations or facades. His own representations of his villa designs, published in his *Four Books of Architecture* (*I quattro libri dell'architettura*), feature orthogonal elevations in the form of woodcuts. The similarity in technique to the facades reproduced here helps us to understand how the villas changed between their conception and the present day. On the other hand, the orthogonal elevation is not without the risk of distortion either, especially regarding the element of depth. If no shading is added to the drawing of a facade, the actual relationships between elements—exactly what is in front of what and by how much—can be open to interpretation. Palladio must have been intrigued by this ambiguous dimension of depth, because he often exploited a compression of depth in his facades.[1] The woodcuts reproduced in his treatise use hatching, or shading by lines, to indicate depth. In contrast, Palladio's drawings in pen, ink, and wash use a much more delicate kind of shading to introduce the element of depth;[2] in this, Giaconi's watercolors are more similar to Palladio's drawings than his woodcuts. The treatment of depth in Giaconi's watercolors is exceptionally effective in allowing us to perceive the villas as three-dimensional objects in spite of their two-dimensional representation. Shadow plays an important role here.

The use of light in Giaconi's watercolors is as important as his use of shadow; his drawings capture the remarkable light of the Veneto that models the forms of the villas, which are shown here with their doors open, as though inviting us to enter. Where the central halls run from the front to the back of the villas, both doors are open, allowing us a view of the clear blue sky beyond, a reminder of the villas' country settings.

All drawings and watercolors were made between 1995 and 2002.

Andrea di Pietro della Gondola (Andrea, son of Pietro the gondolier) was born in Padua on the feast day of St. Andrew, November 30, 1508, in modest circumstances. His father was either a miller or a mason who worked on millstones and delivered his goods by boat, which was probably how he got his name. His grandfather, Vicenzo Grandi, was also a stonemason and sculptor. At age thirteen Andrea signed articles of apprenticeship for six years with Bartolomeo Cavazza in Padua, and seemed destined to follow in the footsteps of his father and grandfather. But two years later he broke his apprenticeship and rejoined his father, who had in the meantime relocated to Vicenza. By the age of sixteen, in 1524, Andrea signed on with a stone carving studio known as the Pedemuro *bottega*, or workshop, whose owners enrolled him in the Vicentine guild of stonemasons. Andrea might have had a prosperous if not brilliant career as a stonemason—there was quite a building boom in those years and the Pedemuro workshop catered to Vicenza's wealthiest citizens—but a major event in Italian history was about to change the course of architectural history in the Veneto and was to have a profound impact on Andrea: the 1527 Sack of Rome.

Renaissance architecture, with its reinvention or "rebirth" of classical forms, had begun in Florence in the early fifteenth century, before spreading to Rome. The devastation of Rome in 1527 when Spanish, German, and Italian troops under the banner of the Holy Roman Emperor swarmed into the city, caused a diaspora of artists and architects from Rome to northern Italy. They brought with them their knowledge of the forms and values of antiquity; and Venetian patrons, eager to commission prestigious palaces in the latest style, abandoned the Gothic- and Byzantine-influenced architecture that had characterized Venice up to that point for the new architecture *all'antica*, "as the ancients did." Among the architects who left Rome for new opportunities in the north were several who were to have a great influence on the young stonemason: Giulio Romano (to Mantua), Michele Sanmicheli (to Verona), Jacopo Sansovino (to Venice), and Sebastiano Serlio (also to Venice, though only temporarily).

Vicenza in the 1520s and 1530s was a hotbed of architectural activity. Sheltered from war by the protective mantle of the Venetian Republic, its wealthy citizens invested heavily in building, a durable and impressive display of both civic and personal pride. Clients of the Pedemuro workshop were both architects and their patrons. One architect who used the Pedemuro workshop was Sanmicheli, whose background was also in stonemasonry and who was learned in classical architecture. Andrea could not help but be influenced by such a contact. But the defining moment in his life came when he caught the attention of one of the workshop's wealthy clients, Gian Giorgio Trissino, a leading intellectual of the day who held architecture in special esteem. Trissino designed his own villa at Cricoli after an early project of Raphael's for the Villa Madama in Rome, and even began a treatise on architecture, which was, however, never completed. Villa Trissino housed an intellectual academy of the kind so in vogue at that time, modeled after the Platonic academies of antiquity, where the sons of the elite would gather to study disciplines such as rhetoric, grammar, logic, astronomy, mathematics, and geography. Students heard lectures in Greek and Latin, studied the classics of ancient literature, composed and performed music, and discussed philosophy. Admission to Trissino's academy was not based on title of nobility, as at some other academies, but on talent, which Trissino must have recognized in Andrea when he met him in the Pedemuro workshop. As Palladio's first biographer, Paolo Gualdo, put it, "Finding Palladio to be a young man of very spirited character and with a great aptitude for science and mathematics, Trissino encouraged his natural abilities."[3]

It is easy to imagine that entrance into Trissino's orbit was truly the turning point in the stonemason's life. Andrea at the time was already an adult, almost thirty years old, a husband and a father. Trissino introduced him to the world of intellectuals and aristocracy, a world from which Andrea's humble origins would have excluded him. Andrea's knowledge of the world widened like ripples in a pond. Trissino took him to Padua, where Andrea met Alvise Cornaro and Daniele Barbaro, both of whom would influence his future writings on architecture. Trissino introduced him to the study of Vitruvius's *Ten Books on Architecture*, the only architectural treatise from antiquity to have survived to the Renaissance. Vitruvius's writings are more than a little obscure (as Raphael wrote, "Vitruvius sheds much light but not enough"[4]) and must have intrigued Andrea; later he would work closely with Daniele Barbaro to illustrate Barbaro's own translation of and commentary on Vitruvius.

In addition to reading Vitruvius with Trissino, Andrea's architectural formation consisted of studying and copying the drawings of other architects, such as Raphael and Serlio. The diligent copying stood him in good stead, for not only did he come to understand architecture *all'antica*, but he developed into an excellent draftsman and filed away drawings that he could retrieve when practical problems arose, adapting ideas of other architects for his own designs. As Andrea's understanding of architecture grew, so did his desire to study the architecture of antiquity in person. Here too Trissino was instrumental, taking Andrea to Rome, where he was able to "see with my own eyes and measure everything with my own hands."[5] What he saw was even better than what he had expected: "Finding [the remains of ancient structures] worthier of study than I had first thought, I began to measure all their parts minutely and with the greatest care."[6]

Trissino not only transformed Andrea from a stonemason to an architect, he ultimately changed his very identity, bestowing on him the name of "Palladio." The name connotes Pallas Athena, the Greek goddess of wisdom, and is probably in reference to a character that Trissino had created in his poem *Italia liberata dai goti* (*Italy Liberated from the Goths*), an archangel whose expertise in architecture helped free Italy from the barbarians.

The story of Palladio's life is told through his architecture. We know of his travels, his commissions, his patrons, and his buildings, and we read between the lines to construct his life story. But very little is actually known of the man. In 1534 he married Allegradonna, the daughter of a carpenter, who was a lady's maid for the wife of one of Palladio's future patrons, Bonifacio Poiana. Allegradonna bore him five children, whom he was able to give an advanced education; one became an architect, another a lawyer; his daughter married well. Two of his sons would precede him in death, victims of the plague. Palladio must have had an engaging and endearing character; he certainly made a good impression on Giorgio Vasari, who met him in Venice in 1566 and wrote of him in *Lives of the Artists* (*Le vite dei più eccellenti pittori, scultori e architetti*): "I won't refrain from saying that in addition to his many virtues he has such an affable and gentle nature that he is most loved by all."[7] Palladio died on August 19, 1580. True to his unassuming nature, he was buried in the family vault, but in the nineteenth century he was reburied in a monumental tomb in the civic cemetery in Vicenza. A statue of Palladio now stands in Vicenza's Piazza Palladio, and the main thoroughfare has been renamed Corso Palladio. But it is perhaps the villas that we see here that are the best memorial to the man.

Palladio as Author

Palladio was not only a prolific architect, he was also a formidable intellect. He was the author of three treatises that are almost unknown today but which shaped the ideas of visitors to Rome for two hundred years after their publication. The first, published in Rome in 1554, was entitled *Le antichita' di Roma* and dealt with the description and history of the monuments of ancient Rome. The second, published the same year, was a guidebook for religious pilgrims to Rome, describing churches, indulgences, and reliquaries. It also included comments about the art found in the churches, the first guidebook of its time to do so. The third of Palladio's minor treatises, published in Venice in 1575, was an edition of Julius Caesar's *Commentarii* on the war with the Gauls (*De bello gallico*), with illustrations by his sons Orazio and Leonida, to whom Palladio dedicated the book after their untimely death during the plague in the 1570s. The study of Caesar resulted not only from Palladio's love for antiquity, but also from his passion for military architecture.

Palladio's most ambitious writing project, however, and the one he never completed, was his treatise on architecture, *The Four Books of Architecture*. He brought to this encyclopedic compendium all his strengths as a professional: his knowledge of detail from his training as a stonemason, his personal study of the ruins of ancient Rome, his excellent draftsmanship, and his own broad experience of design. Palladio set down without academic pretensions his theory of architecture, illustrating it with the designs for his own buildings in their ideal form—that is, without their being compromised by function or site or the intervention of others—along with a practical "how-to" guide intended for those directly involved in the building process. Palladio's straightforward descriptions contrast with Vitruvius's obscurity. Goethe compared the two:

> Since Palladio keeps referring to Vitruvius, I have bought Galliani's edition, but this tome weighs as heavy in my luggage as it weighs on my brain when I study it. I find Palladio, by his own way of thinking and creating, a much better interpreter of Vitruvius than his Italian translator.[8]

First published in Venice in 1570, by Palladio's death in 1580 his treatise was already an international bestseller. Two hundred years later, it had been translated into Latin, Spanish, French, English, German, and Russian. Its influence was tremendous, and created the movement that came to be known as Palladianism. In taking the care to write about architecture in a systematic way Palladio assured his own immortality. In his *Italian Journey*, Goethe described how he bought his copy of the *Four Books* at a bookshop in Vicenza in September 1786:

> There were about a half a dozen people there when I entered, and when I asked for the works of Palladio, they all focused their attention on me...they spoke highly of it and gave me all kinds of information about the original edition and the reprint. They were well acquainted both with the work and with the merits of the author. Taking me for an architect, they complimented me on my desire to study this master who had more useful and practical suggestions to offer than even Vitruvius, since he had made a thorough study of classical antiquity and tried to adapt his knowledge to the needs of our times.[9]

Thomas Jefferson, who was inspired by Villa Almerico, the "Rotonda," for his design of Monticello, is said to have called the *Four Books* "the bible." This is described in a letter dated February 23, 1816, from Colonel Isaac A. Coles to General John Cocke: "With Mr. Jefferson I conversed at length on the subject of architecture. Palladio he said 'was the Bible.' You should get it & stick close to it."[10]

It was through the *Four Books* that Palladianism spread first to England and then to the New World. Palladio's villas themselves were difficult and costly to visit, whereas the book was relatively inexpensive. But while the illustrations in the *Four Books* are valuable records of Palladio's ideals and intents, they cannot always be taken as a literal record of the villas they portray. Palladio intended the *Four Books* to be used as a guide rather than simply a record of his own accomplishments, and idealized the villas for publication.

Villas in Palladio's Œuvre

Writing a succinct account of Palladio's villas is no easy task, as even Vasari admitted in his brief account of Palladio in his *Lives of the Artists*: "all of the works listed above [are held to be very beautiful], and it would have been a very long story if I had wanted to recount the particulars of the beautiful and strange inventions and caprices."[11] A survey of Palladio's work, such as this present collection of watercolors of the villas by Giaconi, shows Palladio's remarkable flexibility and, as Vasari noted, his inventiveness and willingness to derive new formal solutions for the different requirements of the client or different site restraints or features. It becomes evident that his architecture is far from being the result of a formula, though certain principles of architectural form, symmetry, and proportion constitute an underlying regulating system.

What is of immediate interest with regard to architectural form is Palladio's architectural vocabulary, the collection of elements from which the architect composed his designs. Palladio was an architect's architect: he had studied the ruins of ancient Rome, the drawings and design of other architects, and the masterpieces of contemporary architecture to such a degree that he was able to articulate his designs using a precise architectural language.[12] It was in part his use of classical elements that made him, in architectural historian James Ackerman's words, "the world's most imitated architect."[13] A study of the villas allows us to see how Palladio developed and perfected his classical vocabulary, from its most abstract in the early Villa Poiana, to its most literal in the Villa Barbaro in the middle of

his career, to its most "Palladian" in his crowning achievement, Villa Almerico, the "Rotonda."

One of Palladio's regulating principles is symmetry, which is as much at the service of function as of beauty. The one feature that is common to all the villas is their tripartite division, the division of the main body of the villa into three parts. This division is clearly evident on the facades, where the central portion is defined by the formal entrance to the villa, which can take the form of three arches, a *serliana*, or a columned porch crowned with a triangular pediment, and is flanked by symmetrical side elements. What this reflects is not simply an aesthetic preference, but Palladio's attention to structure, for the architect was also a skilled engineer; the tripartite division allows him to place bearing walls in the villa for maximum effect.

Much ink has been used in the debate about Palladio's use of proportion. Although scholars frequently refer to a Renaissance theory of proportion, what exactly proportion meant to sixteenth-century architects is, in fact, not fully understood. Palladio provided some dimensions for rooms in the villas in his *Four Books*, but these are open to interpretation. What is sure is that Palladio believed in a hierarchy of spaces, and allotted space for large, medium, and small rooms around the main hall, or *salone*, of the villa. Proportion determined how high these rooms were according to their width and length. As a result his interiors are perceptibly orderly and harmonic.

Palladio often used his villas as a testing ground for other kinds of architecture, as he apparently felt that he had greater freedom with a country residence than with a city palace. Thus we find that he experimented very early on with the application of a temple front in the Villa Gazzotti and later, as a mature architect, audaciously added a dome to the Villa Almerico, the "Rotonda." But without a doubt Palladio's greatest contribution to the villa as a building type was that, in effect, he defined it as such. Before Palladio, country residences had either been refurbished castles, which were uncomfortable to contemporary tastes, or a haphazard collection of buildings. Palladio created a new kind of agricultural and residential complex that was exactly suited to the needs and wishes of his sixteenth-century Venetian and Venetan patrons. What he could not have foreseen was that the building type he created also proved to be exactly suited to eighteenth-century and nineteenth-century English nobles and Southern American planters. Palladianism has made Palladio's villas not just a Vicentine architecture, but an international style.

There has been almost as much time spent determining exactly what villas are truly Palladian as there has been analyzing them. While Palladio himself described twenty-four villas in his own treatise, his later admirers Ottavio Bertotti-Scamozzi and Francesco Muttoni also assembled books identifying his architecture. Some of these attributions have been contested. Most of the attributions of villas that Palladio did not identify as his own are based on style, such as the Villa Forni, but this can be tricky, because even in Palladio's lifetime his style was imitated. Other attributions have been based on evidence provided by documents and letters, such as Villa Sarego at Cucca. This present collection of the villas of Palladio takes a very broad view of the subject. Of the thirty-two villas presented here, designs for twenty-one appear in Palladio's *Four Books*. (Of the three villas that appear in the *Four Books* but do not appear in this collection, Villa Ragona and Villa Mocenigo at Marocco di Mogliano Veneto were destroyed altogether, and Villa Moccnigo at Dolo was never constructed.) Included here are villas in which, even though Palladio originally designed them, his hand is only barely discernible, such as the Villa Angarano. Also included are villas of which only fragments remain, such as the Villa Porto at Molina di Malo. The collection includes one villa with which Palladio was undoubtedly familiar and on which he may have worked as a stone-mason, but which he did not design: the Villa Trissino at Cricoli. It includes villas that tradition attributes to Palladio, but about which scholars are undecided: the Villa Contarini and Villa Piovene. What this wide panorama allows us is to see many different aspects of Palladio's villas—what came before, works in progress, what came after.

Life in the Villas of the Veneto
The villas we visit today are stately patrician homes, but they were once the centerpieces of whole agricultural complexes, manifestations of a changing economic and social system.

By the early sixteenth century, the growing profitability of agriculture tempted many Venetians to invest in estates on the mainland. While the earliest villas were owned by Venetian nobles, the well-off middle class also came to acquire more and more country holdings. Although some voices were raised in criticism of those who favored agriculture over the traditional mercantile activities of the Venetians, many others sang the praises of country life, much as we do today. Palladio wrote:

> Houses in cities really are splendid and convenient for the gentleman, since he has to live in them throughout the period that he needs for the administration of the community and running his own affairs. But he will perhaps find the buildings on his estate no less useful and comforting, where he will pass the rest of the time watching over and improving his property and increasing his wealth through his skill in farming, and where, by means of the exercise that one usually takes on the country estate on foot or on horseback, his body will more readily maintain its healthiness and strength, and where, finally, someone whose spirit is tired by the aggravations of the city will be revitalized, soothed, and will be able to attend in tranquility to the study of literature and quiet contemplation.[14]

Aside from the villa's function as a place to tend to business, while at the same time providing exercise, relaxation, and entertainment, a house on the mainland also offered a haven from the sweltering heat of the city. The villas were usually inhabited from the middle of June to the end of July, and from the beginning of October to mid-November. In Italian this summer sojourn to the country is called *villeggiatura*, an expression closely related to *villa*.

The term *villa*, which originally encompassed the whole country estate, came gradually to refer to the principal house, a grand country residence—the rural equivalent of the grand city house, the *palazzo*. Its architecture had to reflect the prestige and power of its owners; as Palladio wrote, "The house of the owner must be built taking into account the family and their status in the same way as is customary in towns."[15] But the villa was usually also a working farm, and the architecture often reflected that as well. The grand stepped ramp in front of the Villa Emo, for example, was probably as important for its occasional use as a threshing floor as for its monumental appearance. The villas often combined residential and service functions: kitchens and workrooms in semibasements, which maintained a constant temperature year-round for conserving food and wine; living rooms on the main floor; and granaries and haylofts on the upper floor, under the eaves, where the wind and sun would protect the grain and hay from mildew.

It may surprise modern visitors to the villas to learn how flexible the architecture of the villa was. When we tour the villas today, the guide will often describe the rooms as "living room, dining room, bedroom, sitting room," etc. But in his plans in the *Four Books*, Palladio makes no such distinction between the functions of rooms. The *salone*, or central hall, aside, all of the rooms could be used as the need arose: now a sitting room, now a bedroom, now a study. Sometimes the use made of the rooms varied with the season, as when the warmth of a west-facing room was appreciated in late spring, but made it too hot for sleeping in the summer. Sometimes their use varied according to necessity. Palladio wrote of Villa Ragona, "other rooms . . . can serve as granaries and also as rooms in which to live when the occasion arises."[16] The villas were made all the more flexible by the fact that they were usually sparsely furnished. Often what furniture there was, was brought in by the owner's family when they took up residence for the warm months of the year, and then was moved back out to the city residence when the family returned

to town for the winter. But the centerpiece of the house was the *salone*. Its proportions leave no doubt in the visitor's mind as to its importance: it sometimes runs the full depth of the villa from front to back and is of double height; often it is crowned with barrel or cross vaults, and it is sometimes richly and gaily frescoed. This is where the family held court, entertained visitors, held banquets and balls, listened to concerts, and watched plays.

The country estate was a self-sufficient world of its own. In addition to agricultural fields, there were cutting gardens, vegetable gardens, greenhouses, pleasure gardens, hunting grounds, and fishing ponds. Villa owners were not merely onlookers or overseers but actively participated in the life of the villa. Leonardo Emo, commissioner of Palladio's Villa Emo, for instance, was instrumental in bringing the cultivation of maize to the Veneto from the New World to replace the wheat and barley previously cultivated on his land.

The element that most distinguishes the villas of the Veneto from those of Tuscany, the other region in Italy famous for its villas, is water. Although the mainland of the Venetian lagoon was called *terraferma* ("solid ground"), it was crisscrossed by rivers large and small, and dotted with swamps and bogs. Water management, involving draining fields and reclaiming land for agricultural use, diverting rivers and streams, building artificial canals, and shoring up river banks as protection against floods, was of the utmost importance. Water was the most important means of transportation for people and for goods. Rowing was sufficient to move downstream, whereas horses were used to draw barges and boats upstream against the currents. Most villas were located no more than a few hundred feet from a navigable course of water. Sometimes an approach to the villa was provided by water, and the villa owner on his porch could hail his guests as they neared the villa in their private boats, *burchielli*, used then as we use cars today. In addition to transportation, water was essential for irrigation and for supplying power. Leonardo Emo took advantage of an artificial canal diverted from the Piave River to create a system that cleverly watered his fields according to an eleven-day cycle as well as provided power for the mills to grind the maize he cultivated. Indeed, so well-engineered were the Emo canal and mills that they have been developed continually to the present day and still provide a modest amount of electricity to the villa. Water could also serve another purpose, as at Villa Cornaro; its underground passages brought cold river water to the semi-basement of the villa, where the drafts that it created were funneled up through the rest of the building via the stair towers, providing a sort of air conditioning.

The Villas after Palladio

The economic bubble that permitted the villa building boom in the mid-1500s burst with a serious recession in the late 1500s, and with it ended the era of the villa as Palladio had defined it. When a later generation, in the seventeenth century, was once again able to return to building, the villa was no longer a working farmhouse but a grand country mansion. As far as possible separated from the smelly, messy agricultural functions, the villa became a status symbol, a sign of wealth and leisure. Yet another generation later, luxury gave way to the most conspicuous consumption possible. This transformation of the concept of the villa can be seen in the Villa Contarini, for example, where the original Palladian nucleus has been so transformed and covered with later architectural fashions that it is hardly recognizable today. Perhaps the fate of Villa Contarini is preferable to the disaster that awaited many villas in the nineteenth century, when, after the fall of the Venetian Republic, the economy was on its knees. Villa Foscari, the "Malcontenta," was a victim of hard times, taken over as a barracks for Austrian soldiers, who demolished the *barchesse* and cut down all the surrounding trees for firewood.

Even today, with Palladio recognized for the genius he was and widely studied by scholars worldwide, the villas have not fared as well as one would expect. The most fortunate are still private homes, such as Villa Cornaro and Villa Angarano. Others have been acquired by their municipality and, carefully restored, are open to visitors, such as Villa Poiana, Villa Caldogno, and Villa Thiene (Quinto). Other villas have fared worse. Villa Forni (privately owned but not lived in) is all but ruined, perhaps beyond recovery; Villa Gazzotti (also private, with only parts of the house used for living) is only a little better. Villa Badoer belongs to the province of Rovigo and has been closed for several years for restoration, but a recent visit showed that work has long been halted; the villa was abandoned and unlocked. Villa Emo, still owned by the members of the same Emo family for whom it was commissioned, is intermittently on and off the market, as Count Emo struggles to overcome restrictions on economic activities such as operating a hotel and restaurant that would allow the villa to be financially self-sufficient. These "houses" are in fact very large buildings that are expensive to maintain in the best of circumstances, often requiring extensive intervention to repair the ravages of time and wear; they are, moreover, under strict supervision of the authorities so that permission to intervene is difficult to obtain and repairs made more expensive than usual. Unfortunately, it cannot be taken for granted that because the villas have lasted five hundred years, they will continue to survive.

Visiting the Villas Today

Part of the fun of visiting the villas today is finding them, taking the back roads when possible, driving past fields of grain in the spring and corn in the summer, catching a glimpse of the villas in the distance, only to have them disappear behind a hill, before they reappear in all their splendor when one finally arrives.

In order to find the villas it is helpful to understand how their place names work. Italy is divided into twenty regions, of which the Veneto is one. Each region is divided into provinces, which are much like counties in the United States, with a main city as the *capoluogo,* or county seat. Vicenza is a *capoluogo* in the Veneto. The province is divided into municipalities, or *comuni.* Lugo, for example, is a *comune* in the province of Vicenza. Sometimes the town name is followed by the initials of the province, such as Lugo (Vi). Each *comune* governs both the main town and the outlying villages, which are called *frazioni,* literally "fractions." Lonedo is a *frazione* of Lugo. Thus when we read that Villa Godi is found in Lonedo di Lugo di Vicenza, we know that it is in the *frazione* Lonedo of the *comune* of Lugo in the province of Vicenza. *Frazioni* are usually not shown even on the most detailed of maps, so, when visiting the villas, it is advisable to look for the *comune* and then from there find the *frazione.*

As an architect myself, it was very interesting for me to see that the building techniques used in the roofs and walls of the villas by Palladio are exactly the same as those used currently in Italy. And in writing the text for this book, my own world became more beautiful, for though I have long lived in Tuscany, I but little realized how very much country houses in Italy even today owe to Palladio's designs of five hundred years ago. I hope that the reader's world is likewise made more beautiful.

PLATES

VILLA TRISSINO, CRICOLI
(1532–1538)[17]

The villa that Gian Giorgio Trissino built in Cricoli, on the outskirts of Vicenza, is a mixture of the older tradition of *terraferma* villas and the new architecture of classicism developed by Raphael and his master, Peruzzi. Trissino designed the villa himself, then brought the design to the Pedemuro workshop for its execution. Palladio may have been among those who worked on the villa, which was constructed between 1532 and 1538, when he was an apprentice stonemason at the workshop. Certainly there are elements in this villa that Palladio would later make his own, such as the tripartite arrangement of central halls with symmetrical rooms on either side. But the design of the villa itself may have been of secondary importance to Palladio, because its real significance in his life was that it brought him into the orbit of Trissino and his humanistic academy, transforming him from a stonemason into an architect and one of the leading intellectuals of his day.

Trissino was a rebel, a feudal aristocrat who had dared take a stand against the Venetian Republic in the War of the League of Cambrai in the first decades of the sixteenth century, and who, as a result, was punished by having his land confiscated and being sent into exile. He spent his forced absence in Rome with the Medici Pope Leo X, who later saw to it that Trissino regained his land. Trissino soaked up the humanistic ideals of art and architecture that Leo had brought from Florence to Rome, and in his new villa, took the opportunity to bring these ideals to reality.

The facade, composed of two towers flanking a central body, is all that remains today of Trissino's original design. The simple detailing and massiveness of the towers contrast with the classical orders of the central body, giving the impression of a prince between bodyguards. The towers are in fact remnants from Trissino's previous villa built on the site, holdovers from the earlier tradition of *terraferma* castle-villas. The central body, however, is a primer of Renaissance architecture. Trissino's design is based on an early scheme that Raphael had designed for the garden facade of Giulio de'Medici's Villa Madama in Rome. (Raphael's preliminary design is reproduced in Serlio's 1540 book on architecture, so Trissino may have consulted Serlio as well as Raphael.) The width of the central facade, whose lower part is a screen for the deep-set loggia that provides entrance to the villa, is partitioned into five unequal bays, larger in the center and narrower on the ends. The upper floor features tall windows topped with alternating triangular and arched cornices, and the narrow bays on the upper floor have niches containing statues of Minerva and Peace. Trissino's use of the Ionic order for the lower floor and the Corinthian order for the upper floor reflect his careful study of Vitruvius, a study that he would share with Palladio.

Today Villa Trissino-Trettenero is a private residence. It faces a very busy thoroughfare, which makes it difficult to stop and study the facade. While passersby may ask permission to enter the property to get a better look at the facade, the villa itself is not open to visitors.

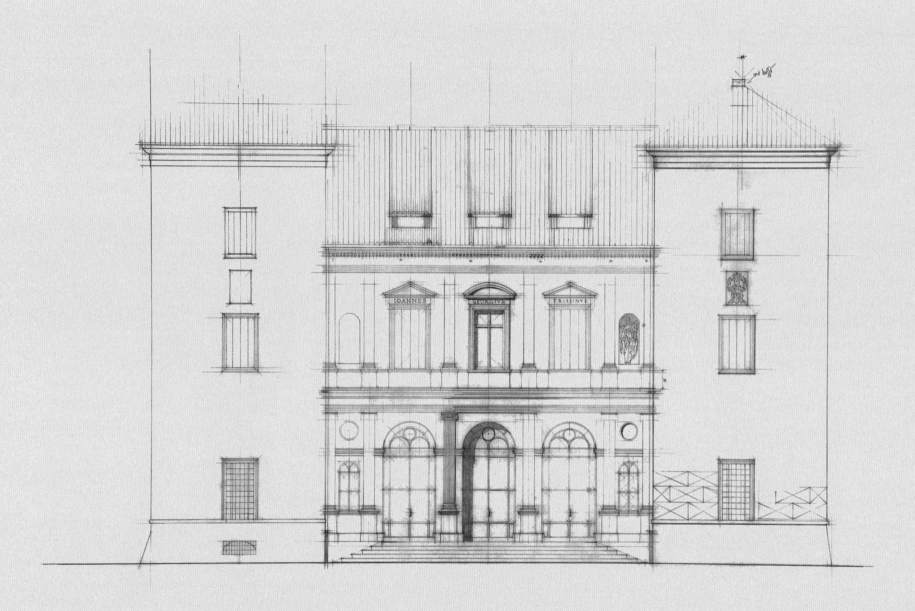

25

VILLA GODI

(1537–1542)

Villa Godi was assigned to Palladio when he was still with the Pedemuro workshop in Vicenza. It was commissioned late in the 1530s by Girolamo Godi, a member of a very wealthy patrician family who had already commissioned the Pedemuro workshop to build other works in Vicenza. Palladio by this time had been with the workshop for more than ten years and was well established, but Villa Godi, the first villa on which he is known to have worked, represents a turning point in his career. Account books prior to Villa Godi identify Palladio as *lapicida*, stonemason, whereas in records of payments made for work on the Villa Godi he is *architetto*.

The villa is located in Lonedo, a *frazione* of Lugo in the province of Vicenza. It is splendidly sited on the high left bank of the Astico River, "placed on a hill with a wonderful view,"[18] as Palladio commented. To make the site suitable for building, Godi had to pay an enormous sum of money to shore up the hillside; the expense was merited, however, as the villa is visible from miles around. It faces onto a garden surrounded by an imposing stone wall, a holdover from earlier *terraferma* castle-villas built when it was too unsafe for a villa to front the open countryside. Palladio would abandon this kind of enclosure in his later villas.

The tripartite division of the villa's facade reflects the division of the interior spaces into three parts—a two-story *salone* flanked by double one-story rooms on either side, the second floor above them intended for use as granaries. This basic symmetrical arrangement of the spaces will appear over and over, refined and perfected, in all of Palladio's villas. Villa Godi's main floor is reached by a stately exterior stair leading to a three-arched loggia, a motif to which Palladio returns time and again. The semi-basement below contains the kitchen and wine cellars. The architecture of Villa Godi, while unmistakably classical in its massing and setting, is plain,

even austere, in its articulation. No architectural order is applied to the facade, that is, no columns or pilasters with capitals and bases inspired by ancient Rome adorn the villa. This essential quality will be seen in others of the early villas: at this stage Palladio had not yet been to Rome, where the details and decorative elements of both the architecture of antiquity and its modern interpretations by contemporary architects such as Bramante would greatly influence his later villas.

But the austerity of the exterior belies the splendor of the interiors, richly frescoed by Giambattista Zelotti, Battista dell'Angelo, and Gualtiero Padovano. In preparation for the frescoes, Palladio returned to work on Villa Godi around 1550 in order to redesign the hall, replacing a thermal window on the garden side with a *serliana*. Girolamo Godi's extravagant spending to shore up the hillside to construct his villa was matched by his expenditure to insure its splendor on the interior. Palladio wrote, "This gentleman, who has the most exquisite taste, has entirely ignored the expense and chosen the most gifted and remarkable painters of our time in order to make it as outstanding and perfect as possible."[19] The names of the rooms reflect the classical subjects of their frescoes: the Arts, Venus, Olympus, the *putti*, the Caesars, and the Triumphs.

The existing villa is significantly different from Palladio's depiction of it in his woodcut for the *Four Books*. Palladio shows the stair spanning the full width of the central block, where today it is narrower, flanked by arches that give access to the lower floor; in his drawing he also raised the central block significantly above the side blocks and crowned it with a triangular pediment. Of particular interest is the spacing of the windows in the side blocks, because it shows Palladio at work on resolving a functional problem: locating the chimneys. The *Four Books* shows three windows evenly placed in each of the side blocks, where in the side blocks of the

actual facade appear four windows. In plan there are two rooms on each side of the *salone*. Each room has two windows with a fireplace between them; thus the outermost windows on each side are relatively close to the corners. Palladio would later write in the *Four Books* that this arrangement was structurally unstable as it risks weakening the building's corners.[20] He found a clever resolution to this problem in the Villa Gazzotti, but the same problem would present itself some twenty years later in the Villa Zeno.

Today known as the Villa Godi-Malinverni and privately owned, the villa has regular visiting hours and can also be visited by appointment.

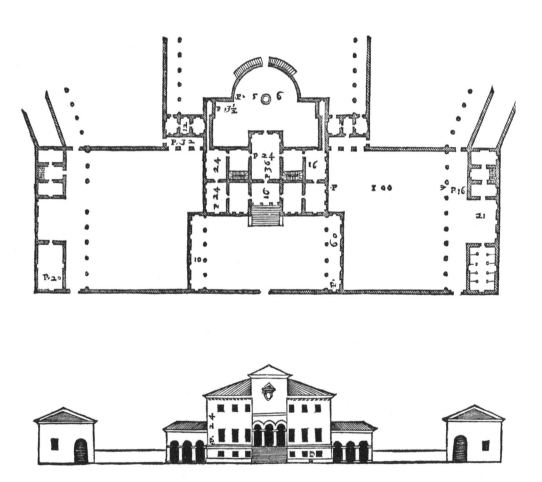

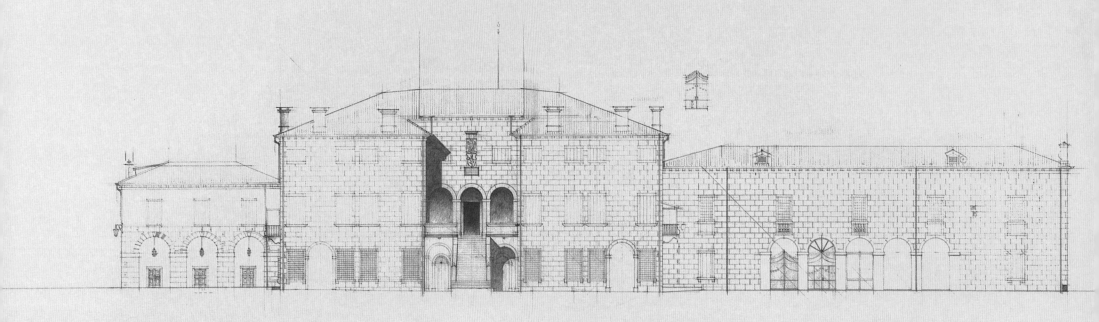

VILLA PIOVENE

(LATE 1530S)

Villa Piovene is located next to the Villa Godi, on the left bank of the Astico River in Lonedo, a *frazione* of Lugo Vicentino. One would think that the Godi and the Piovene were good neighbors, as their villas were so close to each other, but the truth is that they were far from friendly. Indeed, a feud between them continued for generations. At one point a furious Orazio Godi and his men broke into the Villa Piovene to find Fabio Piovene cowering in a wardrobe, and shot him in cold blood. Even Palladio may have been used in the families' battle for prestige, as they vied for the best position and most beautiful estate.

Documentation is scarce on the villa, and scholars are divided as to Palladio's actual role in the villa's design. The villa was most likely commissioned in the late 1530s by Tommaso Piovene, who turned to the Pedemuro workshop for its design. As Palladio was still involved with the Pedemuro workshop, and was working at that time on the Villa Godi, it is presumed that he worked on the Villa Piovene as well, although there is no documentation to prove this. Initially, its simple massing was similar to that of Villa Godi, but its central pavilion projected out beyond the flanking wings rather than setting back. The loggia with its six Ionic columns and proud pediment was begun in 1570 and was probably only based on a design by Palladio and not actually executed by him; it is inscribed with the date 1587. The balustered double stair, the flanking colonnaded wings, and the entry gate were added in 1740 by architect Francesco Muttoni. Muttoni also designed the seemingly endless monumental stair that leads from the gate to the villa. The Baroque style of the stair is emphasized by the statues that line it, which are the work of Orazio Marinali. The garden was designed in the nineteenth century by Antonio Piovene.

Today known as the Villa Piovene Porto Godi, the grounds are open for visits, but the interior is private and cannot be visited.

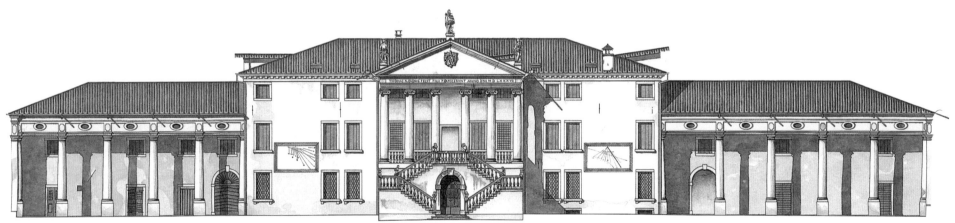

VILLA VALMARANA, VIGARDOLO
(1541–1543)

Villa Valmarana, located in Vigardolo, a *frazione* of Monticello Conte Otto just a few miles north of Vicenza, is attributed to Palladio on the basis of a drawing in the collection of the Royal Institute of British Architects (RIBA).[21] The villa follows the Villa Godi, and its design is the first in which Palladio introduces a specific architectural element from antiquity, the *serliana*, probably a result of his first visit to Rome in 1541 with Gian Giorgio Trissino. Before this trip, Palladio had admired the villa designs of Raphael and Giulio Romano, but his only experience with Roman architecture had been copying the drawings of others. The knowledge that he gained from sketching, measuring, and reconstructing the Roman ruins on paper is clearly visible in his villa designs.

The villa was commissioned by the cousins Antonio and Giuseppe Valmarana. Antonio's father, Pietro, was a friend of Girolamo Chiericati, who also commissioned a villa from Palladio. Construction on the front half of the villa was under way by 1541, but the back half would not be finally completed until some twenty years later. The differences between Palladio's study for the villa and its final built form may be due to this slow building process.

Villa Valmarana is the simplest and most essential of all the early villas, surprisingly modern in its abstraction. It is misleading to say that the villa has a pediment, and rather closer to reality to say that the building *is* a pediment. Its single body has a strong gabled profile, broken only by a very slight setback that creates shadow lines to define the central plane of the entrance. The main element in the facade is the villa's entrance, a *serliana* composed of two rectangular openings flanking a higher central arch. This motif appears in designs by Raphael and Bramante but takes its name from the published designs of Serlio. At the time that Villa Valmarana was designed, Palladio was experimenting with the *serliana* quite a bit: it appears in a drawing of 1540 for a palace design in the collection of the RIBA;[22] in another early study for the design of the Villa Valmarana at Vigardolo, in the same collection[23]; and in 1542 in the vestibule of his first urban palace project, the Casa Civena in Vicenza. A short time later, in 1546, he would exploit it to camouflage imperfections in the arcades of the Basilica of Vicenza. As for its use in villas, it appears in the late 1540s in the loggia of the Villa Poiana; when Palladio returned to the Villa Godi in the mid-1550s, he placed a *serliana* in the rear of the *salone*; and in the 1560s we find it again in the loggia of the Villa Forni. American and English imitators of Palladio would come to associate the *serliana* so exclusively with Palladio that it would become known as a "Palladian window." On the villa's interior, the *serliana* opened to a loggia set back within the body of the house, once completely open and now enclosed by glass doors. The loggia opened to its rear to a small corridor that led to the *salone* beyond. Small, medium, and large rooms symmetrically flanked the central core.

Today Villa Valmarana-Bressan is privately owned and is open to visitors by appointment. It can be rented for weddings and other ceremonial occasions. It was once extensively frescoed by an unknown artist but today only pieces of the frescoes are left.

35

VILLA GAZZOTTI
(1542–1543)

Just about a year after his first visit to Rome, Palladio designed a villa in Bertesina, only about three miles from Vicenza, for Taddeo Gazzotti. Gazzotti was not an aristocrat, but he had married a member of a Vicentine noble family, the Pagelli. He was a man of great culture, with a passion for music and architecture. In 1550, when the villa was still incomplete, Gazzotti went bankrupt, having invested heavily in a deal involving a speculation on salt taxes, which failed. He was forced to sell the unfinished villa to the Venetian Girolamo Grimani, who finished the villa a few years later. Certain details on the facade indicate that the villa was not finished according to Palladio's original design. For instance, the presence of single pilasters at the outermost corners instead of double columns to reinforce the corner (such as in the central block of Villa Pisani at Bagnolo) suggest that the facade was meant to be extended. Also, the entrance stair is too narrow for the porch, and should have extended its full width. Palladio's original intentions for the villa appear in a drawing in pen, ink, and wash in the RIBA collection.[24]

In spite of changes that may have been made to the original design, Villa Gazzotti demonstrates important developments in Palladio's villa designs. Palladio maintains his usual tripartite division of the facade into a central entrance block flanked by side wings and, as at Villa Valmarana in Vigardolo, the central block is set off from the side wings by the slightest of setbacks creating shadow lines. This kind of ambiguity regarding the projection of the central element (does it project or not?) recalls the convention of illustrating buildings as orthogonal representations, that is, in elevations seen straight on in which it is difficult to read depth or projection.

Here for the first time Palladio crowns the central block with a triangular pediment. He referred to his studies of Roman antiquities to demonstrate that the temple with its pedimented loggia was originally adapted from Roman houses, and thus justified the application of the pedi-ment to his villas. From now on the pediment will be a part of all of Palladio's villas, with the notable exception of the Villa Sarego at Santa Sofia.

Here, also for the first time, Palladio applies an architectural order, in this case the Corinthian, to the facade. In addition to making the villa more classical, using the pilasters to subdivide the overall width of the three parts of the facade into regular bays allows him to resolve a problem that he first faced in Villa Godi, that of accommodating the chimneys. Where in Villa Godi Palladio accepted the awkward spacing of the windows in order to place the chimneys in the center of the walls, in Villa Gazzotti the application of the Corinthian pilasters at regular intervals allows the chimneys to coincide with the pilasters, while the windows are evenly spaced in the center of the bays.

In plan, the loggia, covered by a barrel vault, opens to two square rooms on either side. At its rear, it opens to a cruciform *salone* covered by a cross vault, which was probably inspired by the cross vaults Palladio had seen in the Roman baths. He had originally planned a cross vault for the loggia of Villa Valmarana at Vigardolo, which was never built, but cross vaults do appear in the Villa Pisani at Bagnolo and, later, in the Villa Foscari. The *salone* opens to two rooms on either of its sides.

Today known as the Villa Gazzotti-Marcello, the villa is still part of a farm complex in the town of Bertesina. One side of the villa is inhabited, but the other side is used as storage and presents a sad spectacle of decay and neglect. The villa is now under restoration, however. Its exterior is always visible, but the interiors cannot be visited.

Even in its dilapidated state, Palladio's essential classicism shines forth. One wonders whether it is better that the building has survived even to be so neglected, rather than having been altered to the point of being unrecognizable as in the case of Villa Contarini.

VILLA PISANI, BAGNOLO
(1542–1545)

Villa Pisani at Bagnolo, commissioned in 1542 and finished by 1545, was the first villa that Palladio built for Venetian clients, counts (and brothers) Vittore, Marco, and Daniele Pisani. The principal entrance to the villa was from the Guà Canal, a tributary of the Po, and the facade facing the river features Palladio's typical tripartite division, in this case, a central loggia flanked by two towers. The towers are visual references to the earlier *terraferma* castle-villas, and reminiscent of Gian Giorgio Trissino's villa at Cricoli. Unlike the central portion of Villa Trissino, however, which seems tightly compressed between its towers, the loggia of Villa Pisani is nicely framed, its triangular pediment projecting slightly beyond the face of the towers so that it does not appear restricted. The loggia is further distinguished by its bold rustication, contrasting with the unornamented smooth surfaces of the towers. The semicircular stairs that lead up to the loggia are all that remain of an earlier scheme of Palladio's for the villa, in which the loggia took the form of a hemicycle, a semicircular-shaped recess. In his illustrations in the *Four Books*, Palladio often showed a coat of arms or family crest decorating the triangular pediment. In the Villa Pisani there is indeed a coat of arms in the pediment, but it belongs to the Loredan family, subsequent owners of the villa.

Palladio has returned here to the use of the three-arched opening for the loggia of the villa, a device that he knew from the Villa Trissino in Cricoli and he himself first used in the Villa Godi. In Villa Pisani the arch construction is made explicit by the manneristic, rusticated voussoirs, whose design may have been influenced by Giulio Romano's design for the facade of the Palazzo Thiene in Vicenza. The rustication of the voussoirs is repeated on the quoins of the exterior corners of the basement and its windows. The arches are separated by piers in a rusticated Doric order. Double piers define the ends of the loggia, adding to the impression of structural solidity. The piers support an architrave decorated with finely rendered triglyphs, which appear very delicate in comparison to the rustication of the facade.

The loggia opens to the cruciform *salone*, crowned by a cross vault that is richly frescoed with grotesques and scenes from classical myth, reflecting the influence of the Roman *thermae*, or baths. On either side of the *salone* are three rooms of small, medium, and large sizes, a convention to which Palladio returns again and again in his plans. Villa Pisani is the first villa described in Book II of his *Four Books*, where he discusses at some length the proportion of the rooms: "The hall is vaulted and its height is one and a half times its breadth; the vault of the loggias also reaches this height. The rooms have ceilings [i.e. not vaults] and are as high as they are broad; the larger ones are a square and two thirds long, and others a square and a half."[25] Proportion in the Renaissance was very important, as it was a symbolic way of establishing a connection between our human world and the world of the universal and divine. Proportion in architecture was likened to intervals in music. Palladio's use of proportion has been the subject of many a debate, as scholars try to reconcile the theory of proportion in the Renaissance with the various ideas about how that theory may have been applied. In his use of proportion Palladio was anything but dogmatic; absolute proportional values were less important to him than creating a harmonious whole, which is something at which he excelled.

To the rear of the villa is a farm courtyard. While Palladio's plan in the *Four Books* shows *barchesse*, or agricultural wings, on all four sides of the courtyard, only one side exists today.

Villa Pisani had been much altered and was in a dilapidated state until it was thoughtfully and painstakingly restored in the 1970s by the Countess Cornelia Ferri de Lazara, a descendant of the original Pisanis who commissioned the villa. The villa has recently been acquired by the Bonetti family and is open for visits by appointment.

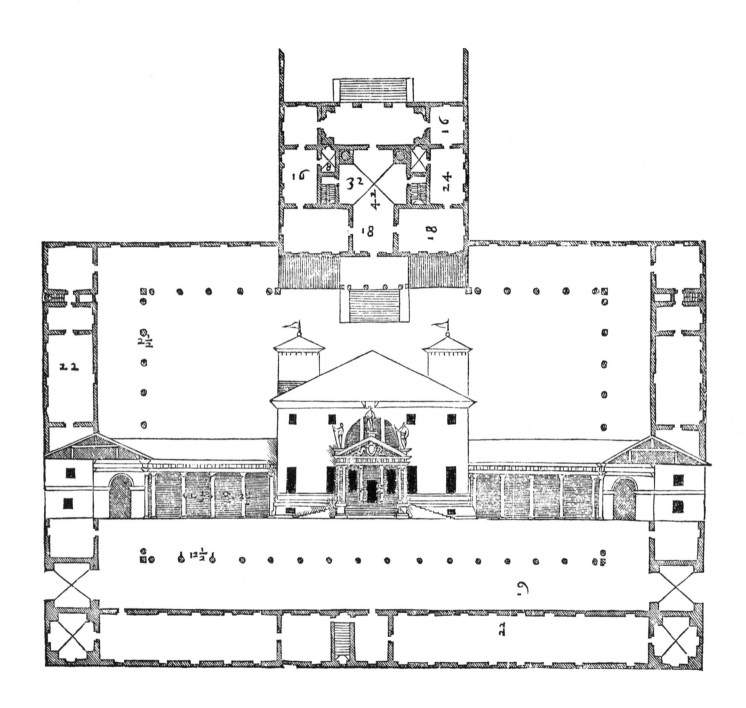

VILLA THIENE, QUINTO VICENTINO
(1545–1546)

In 1542, one of the architects whom Palladio most admired, Giulio Romano, designed a palace in Vicenza for brothers Marc'Antonio and Adriano Thiene. When Giulio Romano died in 1546, Palladio took over the construction on the Palazzo Thiene. In the same year he began construction of a villa for the Thiene brothers in Quinto Vicentino, of which Giorgio Vasari wrote, "At Quinto, near Vicenza, he built...another palace for Count Marcantonio Triene [sic], which is so grand and magnificent that I wouldn't know how else to describe it."[26] Indeed, the Villa Thiene might have become the most magnificent of any of the early villas, except that it was never finished. The portion of the villa that remains today is a powerful indication of the intended grandeur of the original, for what appears to us as a principal facade was actually the side of the villa. We can imagine, then, why Vasari was so impressed!

The villa was originally planned to have a grand principal facade facing the Tesina River, with semicircular steps leading up to a central loggia, very much as at Villa Pisani at Bagnolo. The surprise of this villa is that the loggia would have led to a second loggia, which was open to the rear of the house. From these double loggias the north- and south-facing apartments of the two Thiene brothers were entered. This ingenious solution would have assured both a grand entrance and private quarters for two families. The scheme is shown in a drawing by Palladio now in the Worcester College Library in Oxford.[27] Palladio's later illustration of the villa in the *Four Books* shows an even grander version, with what amounts to two separate villas facing onto a common courtyard, with a U-shaped arrangement of *barchesse* added to house the farm functions.

The north-facing wing for Marc'Antonio Thiene was begun and substantially finished, but construction on the rest of the villa was interrupted when Adriano was forced to flee to France in 1547. At a time when Vicenza was in the grip of the Inquisition, Adriano was suspected of heresy

and feared for his safety. (He was not the only one of Palladio's clients who was a victim of the Inquisition; so was Mario Repeta of the Villa Repeta.) Palladio apparently intended to finish the villa, however; in the *Four Books* he names as his patron Count Ottavio Thiene, who was the son of Marc'Antonio and nephew of Adriano.

Villa Thiene remained unfinished until the mid-eighteenth century, when architect Francesco Muttoni was brought in to modify it. He destroyed the loggia that faced the river to the east and oriented the building towards the north, but preserved the apartments that were already finished. These contain frescoes executed by Giovanni de Mio in the early 1550s. In the nineteenth century the pediment was added, which definitively altered the orientation of the villa. The facade that we see today is divided into alternating narrow and wide bays by flat Doric pilasters, which support an architrave with triglyphs. Small niches for statues are placed in the narrow bays. This arrangement may owe something to Giulio Romano's influence on Palladio (it is found in the Palazzo del Te in Mantua, for instance), but was used by other architects as well, such as Sanmicheli. The alternation produces a livelier visual rhythm in the facade than does a regular column spacing such as that of the Villa Gazzotti.

With the exception of the Doric capitals and bases, the facade is constructed in brick, including the triglyphs in the architrave. Most of Palladio's villas were constructed in brick, then faced in plaster. This is true as well in later villas with round columns rather than flat pilasters, where the columns were built of molded bricks with curved faces. The brick facade at Villa Thiene, then, was never intended to be seen as such, but it does provide an opportunity to see the kind of construction that went into the villas. Today the villa is home to the municipal offices of Quinto, and is open to the public every morning and by appointment in the afternoon.

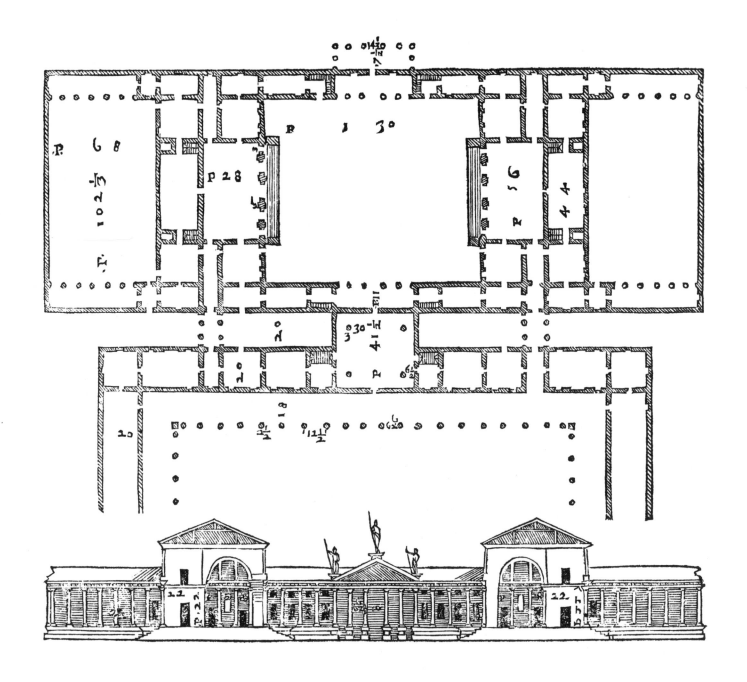

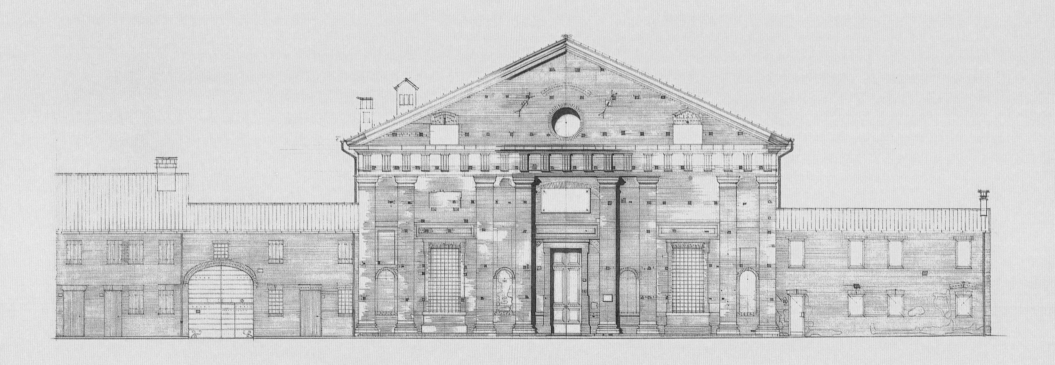

47

VILLA SARACENO
(1545–1548)

Villa Saraceno in Finale di Agugliaro, a municipality some eleven miles south of Vicenza, was built by Palladio in the late 1540s for Biagio Saraceno, an important Vicentine. He was a member of the city council when it was deciding what should be done to resolve the problems of Vicenza's Gothic Palazzo Pubblico (which would come to be known as the Basilica after Palladio's intervention). The council commissioned designs from the leading architects of the day—Sansovino, Serlio, Sanmicheli, and Giulio Romano—but the project for the reconstruction of the building was finally awarded to Palladio. One can imagine that Biagio Saraceno was impressed by Palladio's design for the arcades of the Basilica, and most willingly commissioned the architect to design his own villa in Finale. He was not the only one. The council formed to oversee the construction on the Basilica included members of several of the families who would later commission villas of Palladio: the Angarans, Chiericati, Trissino, Piovene, and Caldogno. This shows us not only how Palladio's fame as an architect spread, but also how intertwined the world of important patrons was.

Villa Saraceno is a compact block, its tripartite facade reflecting the arrangement of small and medium rooms on either side of a loggia and T-shaped *salone* on the interior. As at Villa Gazzotti, the pedimented central portion of the facade is a loggia that barely projects beyond the two flanking portions, just enough to create a shadow line that adds dimension to the facade. The loggia comprises three arches, a motif that Palladio also used in the villas Godi, Pisani at Bagnolo, Gazzotti, and Caldogno. Here, however, the steps leading up to the loggia span its full width. While the other three-arched loggias were intended to have the full-width stairs, Villa Saraceno is the only one built to the original design. The flanking portions have a single window with a triangular pediment at the level of the main floor and smaller square windows with only a simple frame at the upper floor.

The plan of the Villa Saraceno is very simple, with small rooms flanking the loggia and larger rooms flanking the *salone*. As Palladio tells us in the *Four Books*, "the larger rooms are a square and five-eighths long and as high as they are broad; they have ceilings,"[28] that is, they have flat, beamed ceilings and not vaults. The woodcut in the *Four Books* shows *barchesse* placed symmetrically about the central block in a U-shape, but only that to the villa's left was constructed. Almost nothing of the original interior survives, except for a fresco by an anonymous artist in the barrel vault of the loggia.

As at villas Caldogno and Gazzotti, Palladio uses a continuous flat string molding to unify the flanks and the loggia into a single composition. A variation here is that the stringcourse is ingeniously transformed into keystones over the three arches of the loggia, adding a mannerist touch to an otherwise almost completely unadorned facade. The facade was, however, originally less plain than it appears today, as shown by traces of incised lines once meant to represent rustication.

After Biagio Saraceno's death in 1562 the villa remained incomplete. In recent times it was much degraded until it was bought by Britain's Landmark Trust, which carefully restored it and now makes it available for vacation rentals. The villa is also open to visitors.

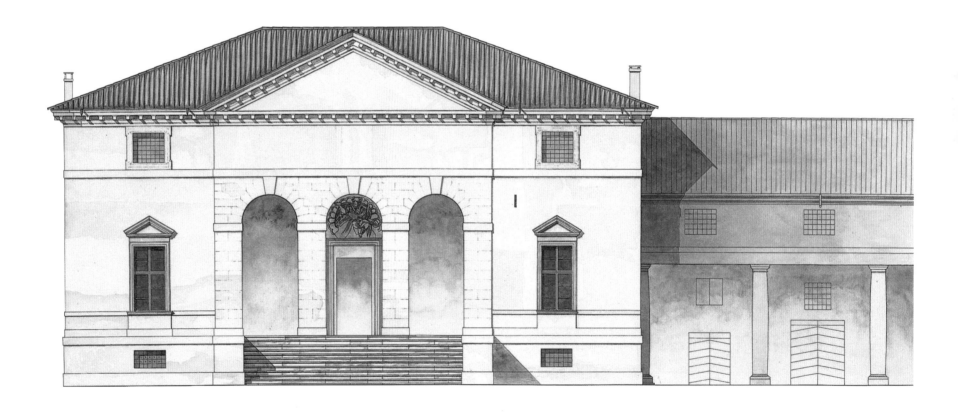

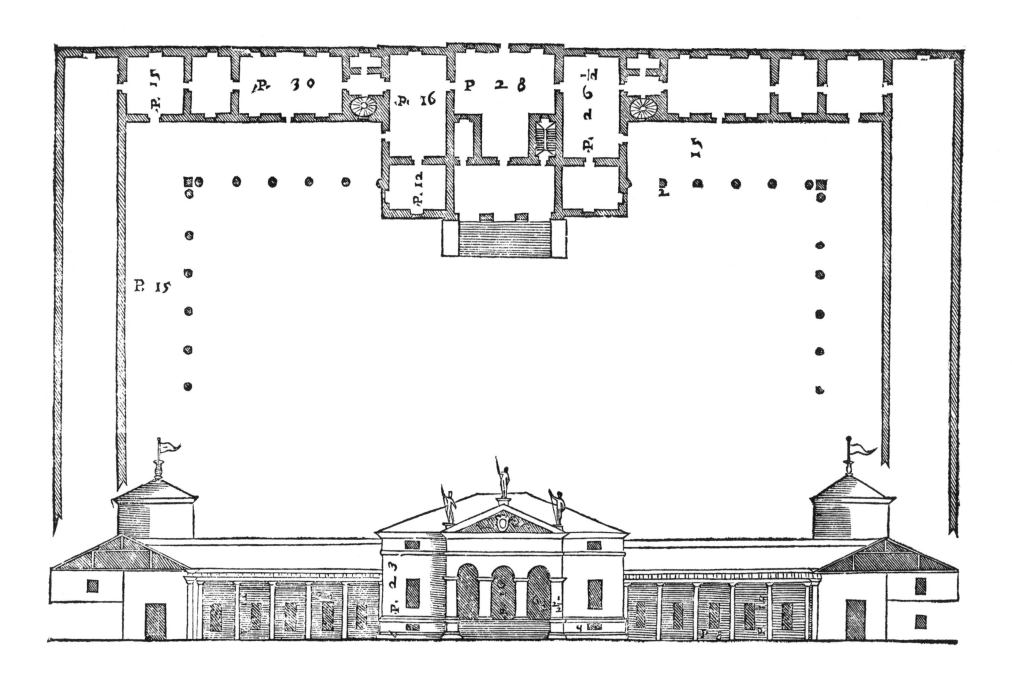

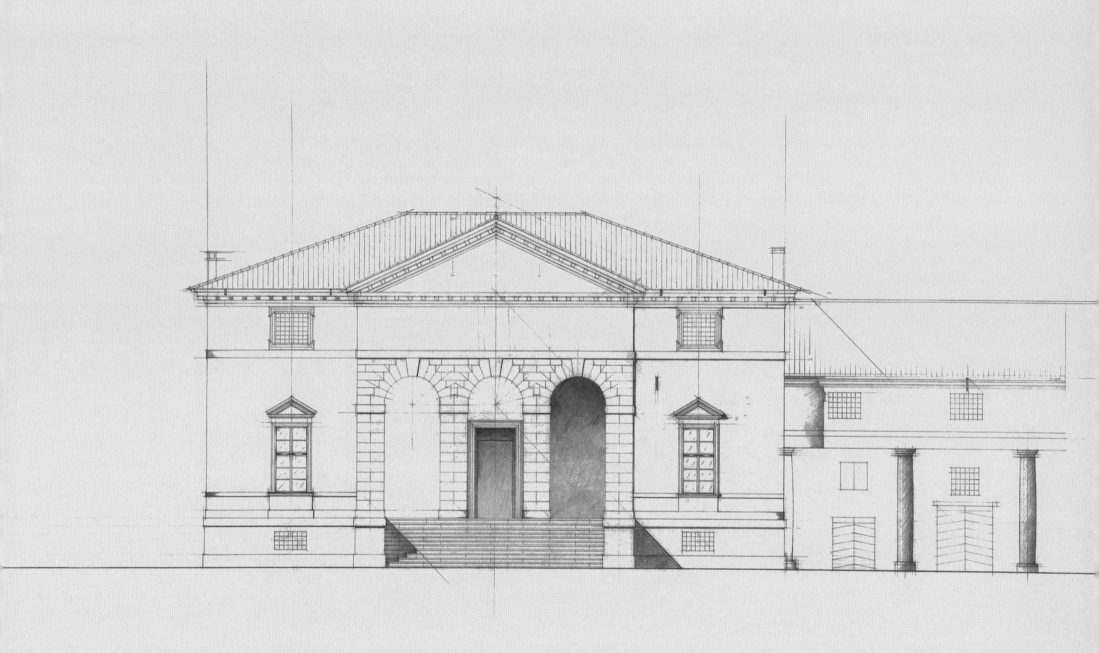

VILLA ARNALDI
(1547–1556)

Villa Arnaldi, if a villa we can call it, was designed for Vicenzo Arnaldi, a Vicentine nobleman. It is in Meledo Alto, a *frazione* of Sarego, some twelve and a half miles from Vicenza and just a few miles from Villa Pisani at Bagnolo. Vicenzo Arnaldi owned an existing farmhouse, and in 1547 commissioned Palladio to renovate it. Drawings for the renovation by Palladio exist, but the actual construction was limited to the beginnings of a three-arched loggia. Vicenzo abandoned the project in 1565, and the house has remained to this day as it was—a rather ramshackle, haphazard farmhouse with the silhouette of the arches, now filled in, still visible. Enough remains of the loggia to allow us to recognize Palladio's hand. Its three arches are flanked by lower rectangular openings on either end, forming a sort of elongated *serliana*. Flat moldings serving as upper lintels for the rectangular openings, and spring lines for the arches provide horizontal continuity. The loggia would probably have been similar to that of Villa Saraceno, where flat moldings also provide a horizontal visual reference as well as spring lines for the arches.

The placement of the loggia on the far end of the body of the house indicates that Palladio planned to build another wing to accommodate his preferred three-part facade and plan. The frames of the windows also are typical of Palladio.

Projects involving the restructuring and incorporation of existing structures were not unusual for Palladio, who faced this task in Villa Godi, Villa Gazzotti, and Villa Barbaro, to name three. Sometimes the existing building would show itself in subtle ways, such as in minor aberrations of room sizes that contrast with Palladio's formal hierarchy. This is the case in Villa Caldogno. Sometimes the existing structure shows itself in more obvious ways, such as the medieval base upon which the Villa Badoer is built, allowing Palladio to gain height for the villa and adding to its imposing character.

In its incomplete state, Villa Arnaldi provides an opportunity to see the kind of existing structures Palladio had to deal with, and gives insight into the process by which he was able to take a nondescript masonry structure and turn it into a "villa." Villa Arnaldi today is privately owned.

VILLA CALDOGNO
(1548–1552?)

When, in the early 1540s, Vicentine aristocrat Losco Caldogno acquired an estate in Caldogno, some four and a half miles north of Vicenza, he asked Palladio to redesign the existing house. Palladio did not publish the project for the Villa Caldogno in the *Four Books*, but a sketch of his in the RIBA collection shows his original layout for the villa, which is compact and simple.[29] The loggia opened to medium-sized rectangular rooms on either side, and to the large *salone* beyond, which, in turn, opened to the smaller rectangular rooms and two narrow spaces on either of its sides (one of the narrow spaces contained the stairs to the upper floor). Having to retain existing parts of the preexisting house prevented Palladio, however, from establishing the hierarchy of small, medium, and large room sizes that usually characterizes his plans. The plan as built comprises two equal rectangular rooms separated by one smaller rectangular room on each side. In the seventeenth century two projecting stair towers and a terrace were added to the rear of the villa, destroying the integrity of the villa's square plan.

The facade shows developments of ideas that Palladio was experimenting with in other villas of the mid-1540s. The very subtle projection of the central body of the facade, the flat string molding to unite the three portions of the facade into a single composition, the triangular pediment over the central portion, and the three-arched loggia are very similar to Villa Saraceno. The articulation of the central portion of the facade by means of a bold rustication, the manneristically exaggerated voussoirs of the three arches with the dropped keystones, and the simple flat pediments of the lateral windows are similar to Villa Pisani at Bagnolo. Even the curiously shaped stair leading up to the loggia recalls the Villa Pisani, though the stair is semicircular there whereas it is semi-octagonal at Villa Caldogno.

In the late 1560s, more than twenty years after Palladio's initial involvement, Losco's son Angelo again wished to renovate the villa, but it is unclear whether Palladio was involved in the second remodeling. Angelo would certainly have kept Palladio in mind, for not only had his father commissioned him, but Angelo was married to the daughter of Marc'Antonio Godi, brother of Girolamo Godi for whom Palladio built the Villa Godi. One visible sign of Angelo's work on the villa can be seen in the string molding above the three-arched loggia, where an inscription reads ANGELVS CALIDONIVS FILIVS MDLXX, "Angelo Caldogno the son 1570."

Angelo Caldogno spared no expense on the decoration of the villa's interiors, which, fortunately, have survived the centuries. The beautiful frescoes are by Giambattista Zelotti and Giovanni Antonio Fasolo, both of whom had worked on other buildings by Palladio—Zelotti in the Villa Godi, Villa Emo, and Villa Foscari as well as several of the large palaces in Vicenza, and Fasolo on the ceiling of the *piano nobile* in the Loggia del Capitaniato in Vicenza. The carved fireplaces are by Lorenzo Rubini, who executed the statues on the staircase in Villa Almerico, the "Rotonda."

The villa today is found in the center of the town of Caldogno, not far from the municipal building, and is owned by the municipality. The restored *piano nobile* is used for exhibitions and conferences and is open for visits from March through October. The semibasement has been beautifully renovated and now houses a public library, which is open year-round.

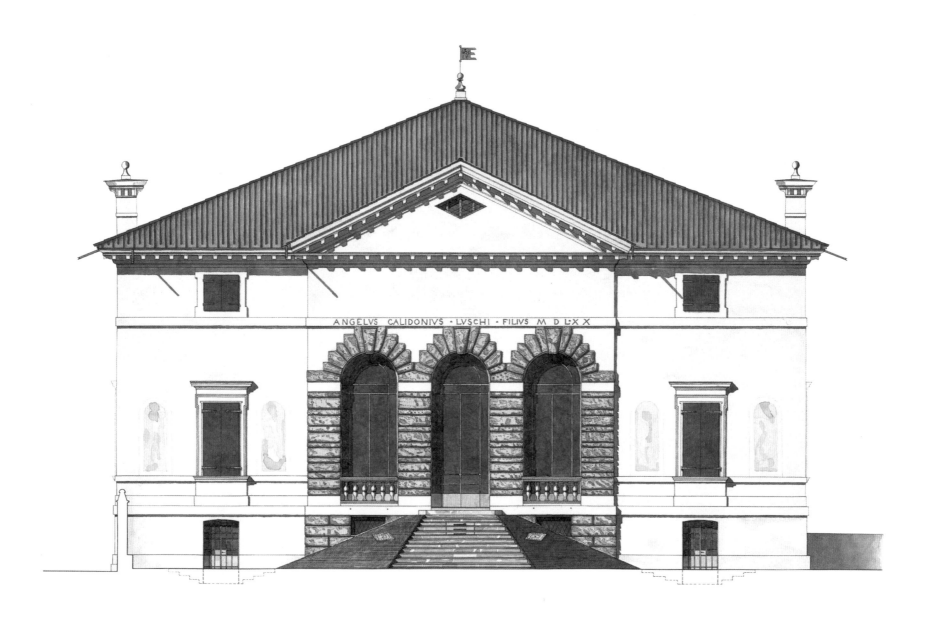

ANGELVS · CALIDONIVS · LVSCHI · FILIVS M · D · L · X · X

VILLA POIANA
(1548–1556)

Villa Poiana was built for Vicentine nobleman Bonifacio Poiana. Poiana and his wife, Angela, had known the architect as a young stonemason, at the time when Palladio's future wife, Allegradonna, was a lady's maid to Angela. Relationships between the two must have been affectionate, as Angela Poiana gave the young bride a dowry upon her marriage to Palladio. Palladio compliments Cavaliere Poiana in his description of the villa in the *Four Books*: "This gentleman, as befits someone of his magnificent and elevated character, has done everything he could to produce all those beautiful and practical things to make his house attractive, pleasing, delightful, and convenient."[30] The villa was commissioned in the late 1540s, but it took some fifteen years to complete its frescoes and statues.

The facade of the villa is divided into three parts, with the central portion given over to a rectangular loggia, which is entered through a *serliana*. The *serliana* acts not merely as an entrance motif, however, but is also a unifying device, the arched form being carried through the villa. The loggia is covered by a cross vault, so the circumference of the central arch on the front wall of the loggia reappears on its back wall; on the interior, the same circumference defines the width and height of the barrel vault that covers the *salone*. The arch then reappears in a *serliana* on the rear facade of the villa, which differs slightly from the front facade, as it contains added windows on the mezzanine and upper levels. This was admissible because Palladio considered the rear facade more functional than formal.

The design of the facade harks back to Palladio's preliminary sketch for the Villa Valmarana at Vigardolo, now in the RIBA collection.[31] At Villa Poiana the *serliana* is embellished by five oculi, or round openings, placed radially over the central arch, a development of the two oculi over the rectangular openings in the *serliana* of Villa Valmarana. The crowning element of the central block of the villa is a broken pediment, a device that Palladio

planned but never realized for the Villa Valmarana, but which does appear on the garden facade of the Villa Foscari, the "Malcontenta."

The interior is richly decorated with fresco cycles by Bernardino India and Anselmo Canera. The walls and cove vaults of the room to the right of the entrance, surprisingly well preserved, are dedicated to the Roman emperors by Anselmo Canera. Small rooms on either side of the *salone* were decorated by Bernardino India with landscape scenes and grotesques, decorative frescoes so named because they were used to decorate the grottos of the villas of antiquity. India would later work on the frescoes in Villa Foscari. For the fireplaces Palladio also acknowledges the participation of stuccoist Bartolomeo Ridolfi of Verona, who would later execute the fireplaces in Villa Almerico.

It is interesting to note the three statues on the pediment of the facade, a late addition by Girolamo Albanese in 1658. Although in the *Four Books* Palladio showed statues (on special pedestals called acroteria) for virtually all of the villas that had triangular pediments (with the exceptions only of Villa Godi and the lost Villa Ragoni), only Villa Poiana, Villa Chiericati, Villa Almerico, and Villa Valmarana at Lisiera actually have them. (Villa Porto at Vivaro and Villa Piovene also have statues, but these are not in the *Four Books*.)

A comparison of the villa as built with the plan published in the *Four Books* shows that the actual construction was very close to the design, except for the outermost wings shown in Palladio's drawing. These wings were not *barchesse*, which are also part of the project, but wings that contained other living spaces. The one wing that was ever built (on the left as one faces the villa) was not added until late in the 1500s, after Palladio's death. The presence of these additional wings on either side of the main body distinguishes Villa Poiana from the villas Palladio designed earlier

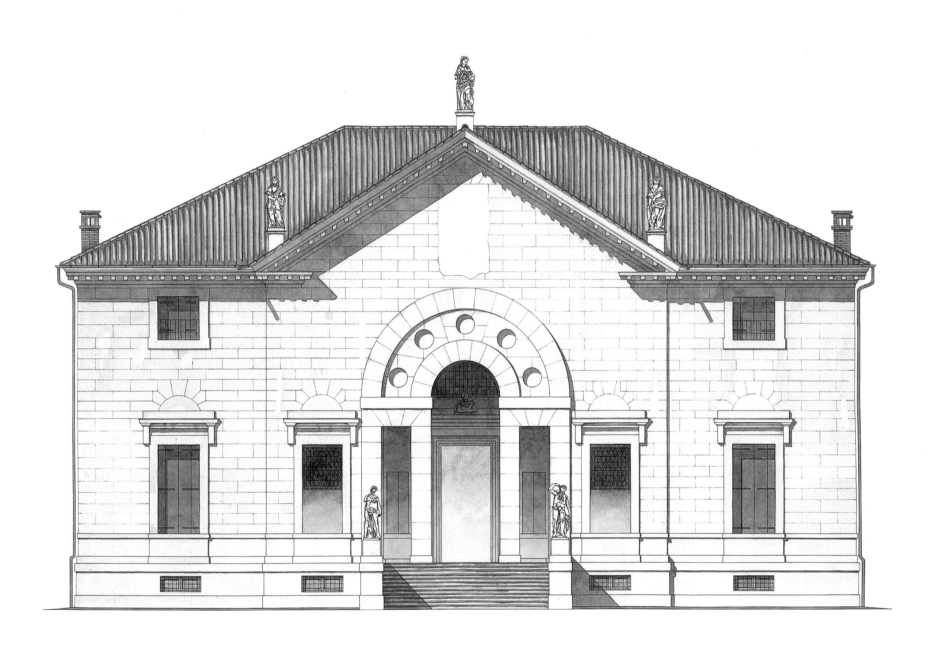

(such as Villa Godi, Villa Pisani, Villa Thiene at Quinto, and Villa Saraceno), and link it to several of the villas designed after it (Villa Cornaro, Villa Thiene at Cicogna, and Villa Valmarana at Lisiera). By the end of the 1540s, when Villa Poiana was designed, Palladio was well established, his fame having spread beyond Vicenza to Venice, Verona, and beyond. The development of the plan and the assuredness with which Palladio handles the arrangement of the rooms, their vaulting, and the articulation of the facade all mark Villa Poiana as a transitional villa in his repertoire and provide a taste of what will come.

At one point Villa Poiana was abandoned and had fallen into almost total ruin, but today it belongs to the municipality, which has carefully restored it. It provides an excellent opportunity to view the structure of the villas, because all levels are open for inspection: the semibasement with its brick vaulting, where a grille in the pavement of the *salone* permitted the cool air from below to circulate into the villa's interior; the *piano nobile*; the mezzanine with rooms for the servants; the lofty attic under the eaves. Of particular interest is the attic, where the shallow vaults and brick relieving arches that support the cove ceiling of the rectangular room below have been left exposed. A visit to the attic also explains the very visible patch under the pediment on the facade. From the attic this can clearly be seen to have been an opening, not in the original project, which is now closed.

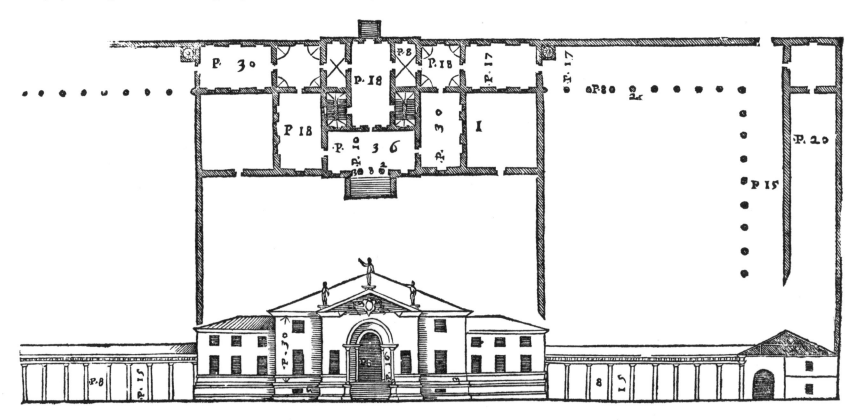

The commissioner of Villa Angarano was one of the patrons that Palladio most esteemed, so much so that he dedicated the first two of the *Four Books* to "my most noble lord worthy of the utmost respect, Signor the Count Giacomo Angarano."[32] Count Angarano was a Vicentine nobleman who owned a large estate in Angarano, a *frazione* of Bassano del Grappa, a good-sized town about nineteen miles northeast of Vicenza. Angarano commissioned the villa in 1548, and he met Palladio in person three times on the site to discuss the design. These meetings were the beginning of a close friendship as well as a working relationship.

Work on the Villa Angarano began with the construction of the *barchesse*, the agricultural wings that were to accommodate the farm functions of the villa. While the *barchesse* were completed, the rest of his plan as published in the *Four Books* was never built. Originally, the *barchesse* flanked a simple farmhouse; this was replaced by the existing grand manor house some 150 years later. Of Palladio's grand design, only the functional structures remain.

In order to understand why a patron would begin work on a prestigious project by first building a structure that was functional rather than formal or a "status symbol," it is important to consider the larger function of the agricultural wings, which was to organize and define the villa site as a whole. Palladio incorporated the *barchesse*, in one form or another, in almost all of the villas shown in the *Four Books* (the exceptions are Villa Cornaro, where the presence of the villa designed by Sanmicheli right next door would have precluded the construction of *barchesse*; Villa Pisani at Montagnana; Villa Foscari; Villa Sarego at Miega; and Villa Almerico, which Palladio does not classify as a villa, since it has no farm functions). In fact, Palladio went so far as to show *barchesse* with villas where site restrictions would not have permitted their construction, such as the Villa Godi and the Villa Pisani at Montagnana. His aim in the *Four Books* was to minimize the site imperfections and limitations, and to illustrate the design of entire villa complexes. To this end the *barchesse* were the perfect means.

The *barchesse* at Villa Angarano were realized in the Doric order. For Palladio, the architectural orders each had their own character and proper application. The Tuscan order, for example, Palladio called "rough": "Tuscan...is rarely used above [the] ground [level], apart from in single-story buildings such as the covered outbuildings in farms."[33] In addition to its sturdiness, Palladio liked the Tuscan order for functional buildings such as *barchesse* because the wide spacing between the columns was convenient for maneuvering carts and wagons. The fact that Palladio chose the Doric order for the *barchesse* in Villa Angarano is a sign that he was building on a grander scale than the functional aspect alone would have required.

It may surprise us that Palladio would consider a utilitarian structure an object worthy of aesthetic considerations, but one of his strong points is that not even the most functional part of the whole design is seen as negligible. Of the *barchesse* Palladio wrote:

> The covered outbuildings for items belonging to the farm should be...connected to the owner's house in such a way that he can go everywhere under cover so that neither rain nor the blazing summer sun would bother him as he goes to supervise his business; this arrangement will also be of the greatest use for storing wood...and the infinite variety of other objects belonging to the farm...; besides which these porticoes are extremely attractive.[34]

Villa Angarano is now the Villa Bianchi Michiel, and is private. It can be visited upon request.

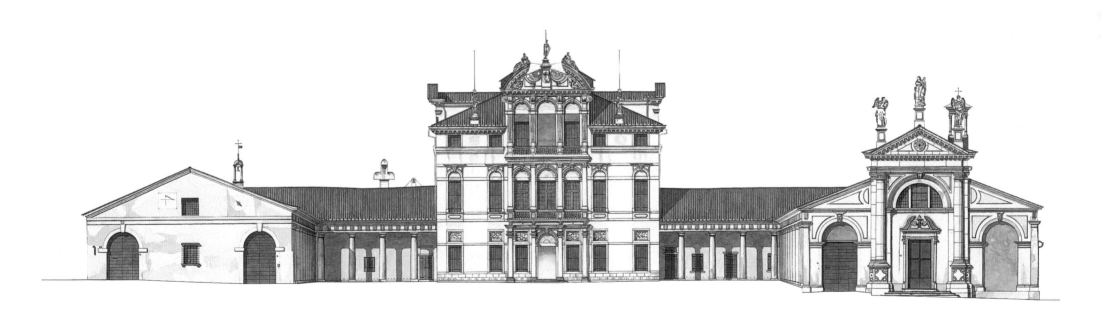

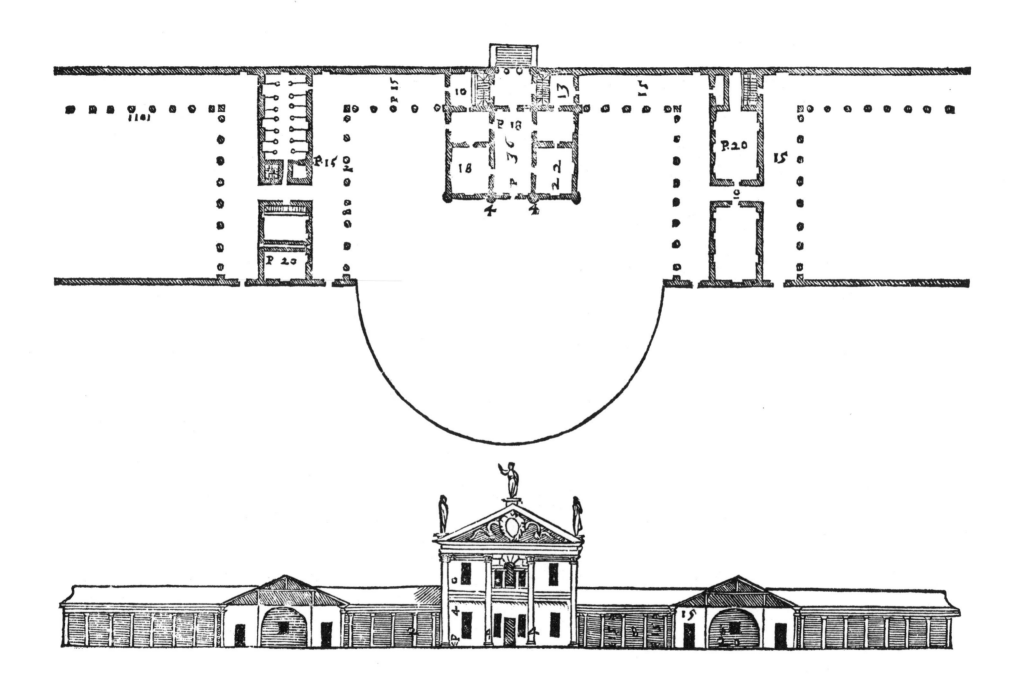

VILLA CORNARO
(1551/2–1555)

Villa Cornaro-Gable in Piombino Dese, on the road from Venice to Castelfranco Veneto in the province of Padua, represents a quantitative leap from the single-story villas that preceded it in the 1540s. Palladio's circle of patrons had grown from the nobles of his own Vicenza to those of Venice and Verona, and accordingly, the budget for the villas had grown as well as the need for appropriate symbols to express the owner's status. Villa Cornaro with its two *piani nobili*, or living floors, was designed by Palladio as a villa-palace, part rural estate, part urban residence, its location on a farm not at odds with its proximity to what was even in 1551 a public thoroughfare and is today a heavily traveled provincial road. The patron was Giorgio Cornaro, whose grandfather was the brother of Caterina Cornaro, former queen of Cyprus. The villa was commissioned in 1551. Construction began in 1552, and the villa was habitable, if not complete, by the time of Giorgio's marriage in 1554.

The facade of the villa features the usual tripartite division, the central part given over to a two-story, pedimented loggia, whose sides are not completely open, but are realized as walls with arched openings. The outermost columns engage the ends of these walls in an arrangement known as columns *in antis*. Palladio had seen this arrangement in the Portico of Ottavia in Rome, a drawing of which, in his hand, is now in the collection of Vicenza's Museo Civico.[35] On the lower *piano nobile*, six Ionic columns support the architrave upon which rest six Corinthian columns of the upper *piano nobile*. These, in turn, support an architrave and triangular pediment. This arrangement of a two-story loggia with a pediment was not unknown in villas of the Veneto, but Palladio brought it to new refinement. In elevation, the entrance facade and the garden facade are almost identical (except for the arrangement of windows in the central portion); when seen in three dimensions, it is obvious that the entrance loggia projects well beyond the central core and its flanking wings, while the garden loggia is recessed into the body of the house.

Villa Cornaro was planned with wings on either side of the central body of the villa to house service functions. It is likely that at least the west wing was begun in the original building program; both were completed about 1590. The addition of the wings creates a greater formal hierarchy and richer overall composition for the villa. As in earlier villas, Palladio uses horizontal moldings to unify the wings with the loggia. In Villa Cornaro, Palladio takes the horizontal lines of the lower architrave as references and carries them as moldings right across the wings. The surface treatment of the villa is also noteworthy. Deeply raked lines in the *intonaco* imitate stone joints. This was a kind of surface treatment that Palladio used on palaces, such as the Palazzo da Porto Festa in Vicenza. Its use on the Villa Cornaro underlines the hybrid villa-palace nature of the building. While Palladio had used lightly etched lines on earlier villas, such as Villa Poiana, these were much less effective as they cannot be read from a distance. Villa Cornaro is unique in that it is the only villa that still has its original *intonaco*, complete with graffiti dating back to the seventeenth century. The graffiti on the walls of the garden loggia record births and calculations. More graffiti, including drawings of a duck and fashionable shoes, can be found in the granary of the uppermost floor where a garrison of soldiers was housed at one time in the seventeenth century.

This is one of the few villas that Palladio planned without *barchesse*; he could not have built them even if he had wished to, because the Villa Cornaro was sited right next to the villa designed by Michele Sanmicheli for Giorgio Cornaro's father, Girolamo, and inherited by his older brother Andrea.

The plan of Villa Cornaro is an elaboration of the plan with which Palladio had experimented for the Villa Chiericati. On the interior, a

relatively narrow entry hall leads from the entrance loggia to a grand *salone* with four free-standing Ionic columns supporting a painted, beamed ceiling. Continuity between the front and back of the villa is provided by the columns of the *salone*, which are aligned with the penultimate columns of both loggias. Large, medium, and small rooms flank the hall and *salone*, which in its turn opens to the garden loggia. Stairways on either side of the garden loggia lead down to the semibasement, and up to the mezzanine rooms for servants above the small rooms, then to the second *piano nobile* for the villa's owners, and finally to the storage spaces under the eaves. Palladio's *Four Books* shows the twin stairs as ellipses, but in fact they are much more easily constructed ovals, with parallel side walls and rounded ends. The upper *piano nobile* is identical in plan to the lower, except that there are no columns in the upper *salone*.

Villa Cornaro's upper *salone* is unfrescoed, but six niches in the corners hold statues by sculptor Camillo Mariani (executed in the early 1590s) of illustrious members of the Cornaro family. The frescoes on the lower floor were painted in the eighteenth century by Mattia Bortoloni and contain many curious references to Masonic symbolism and themes. Stucco work in the villa was done in 1716 by Bortolo Cabianca.

Only the presence of a grass-covered, seven-arched bridge evidences the importance of the waterway, now diverted, that once passed behind the villa and provided an important mode of transportation. Water from the river was brought into the house via underground passages, which may also have provided cool air for the villa.

Today, the villa's private owners have taken important steps to preserve its structure and beauty. The grounds and lower *piano nobile* are open by appointment to visits by groups.

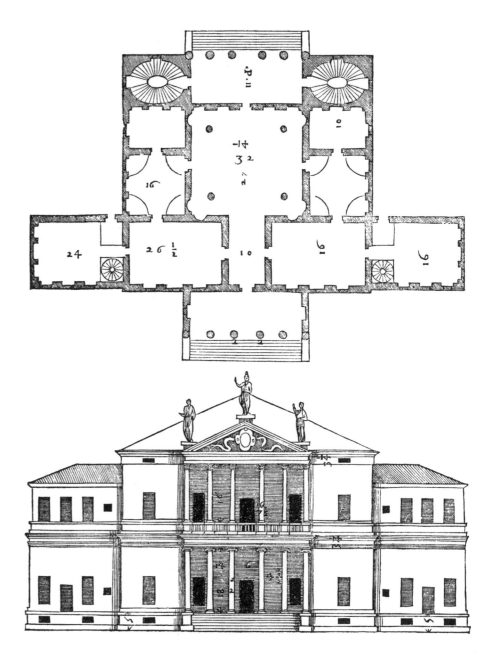

71

VILLA PISANI, MONTAGNANA
(1552–1555)

Francesco Pisani was another of the expanded circle of very wealthy Venetian noblemen who commissioned villas of Palladio in the 1550s. Pisani, who belonged to a different branch of the family than those who built the Villa Pisani in Bagnolo, may have heard of Palladio through his cousins Daniele and Marc'Antonio Barbaro, patrons and mentors of Palladio.

Villa Pisani was built just outside the walls of the medieval town of Montagnana. Designed and built at the same time as Villa Cornaro in Piombino Dese, and in many ways similar to it, Villa Pisani is a villa-palace, a hybrid of country estate and urban residence. Its flattened entrance facade, with applied rather than free-standing columns, is a two-dimensional rendering of Villa Cornaro's more plastic two-story temple front projecting out beyond the flanking wings. In this sense it is more urban than Villa Cornaro, constrained by being right upon the street line, where Villa Cornaro's small garden allows the villa more room to expand. The architectural orders of Villa Pisani's temple front are also more restrained than at Villa Cornaro: here there are four columns on each level as opposed to Villa Cornaro's six. Palladio's use of the architectural orders was never casual. In the *Four Books* he describes them in the order of their strength and refinement, Tuscan, Doric, Ionic, Corinthian, and Composite, writing, "They must be distributed in buildings with the strongest at the lowest position."[36] In keeping with this, we find the Doric order on the lower level here and the Ionic on the upper, whereas at Villa Cornaro, the Ionic order appears on the lower level and Corinthian on the upper.

Palladio's usual device for unifying the central portion with the flanking wings, a continuous horizontal molding, is elaborated here by extending the Doric architrave of the lower order of the loggia—its frieze with triglyphs and metopes decorated with *bucrania*, or sculptured representations of ox heads—all the way around the villa. The villa's facade was originally less uniform than it appears today, as lightly incised lines gave an impression of ashlar coursing or rustication, only very slightly visible now.

The entrance loggia opens directly onto the villa's main public space, which Palladio called the "entrance," as he reserved the term *salone* for the space on the upper *piano nobile* immediately above it, meant for the private use of the residents. The entrance is extraordinary, with intersecting barrel vaults supported on corner arrangements of free-standing and engaged Doric columns. Sculptures of the Four Seasons by Alessandro Vittoria, who also executed the stucco decoration for the pediment over the entrance, decorate this room. Vittoria would later execute the original reliefs for the facade of Villa Forni. A narrow passageway connects the entrance to the garden loggia, which is recessed into the body of the villa and is flanked by twin stairs, as at Villa Cornaro. The plan of the upper *piano nobile* is the same as the lower, but its ceilings are beamed rather than vaulted.

Viewing the villa from the street at its rear reveals that one of the sides of the building actually bridges the moat of Montagnana. At one time this waterway powered a mill and provided income for Pisani.

Palladio's illustration of the villa in the *Four Books* shows a more elaborate arrangement, with flanking towers for service spaces connected to the main body of the house by covered passageways over arches. These were never built, and indeed, given the site restrictions, could never have been built. The idea of these towers, however, served as the model for the wings added in the nineteenth century to the Villa Porto at Vivaro.

Today the villa is known as the Villa Pisani-Placco. It is privately owned and can be visited by appointment.

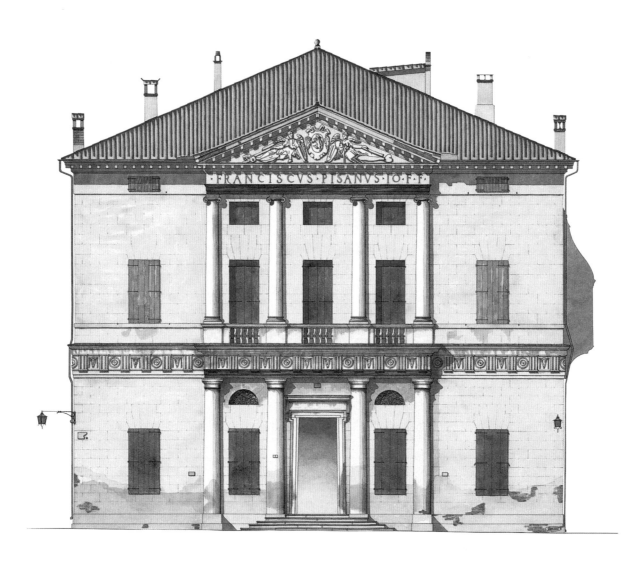

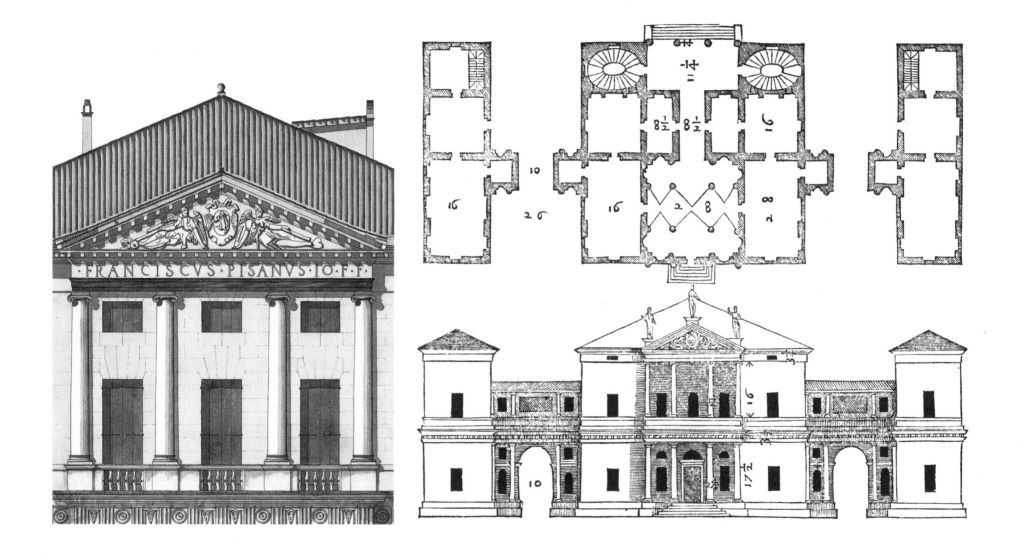

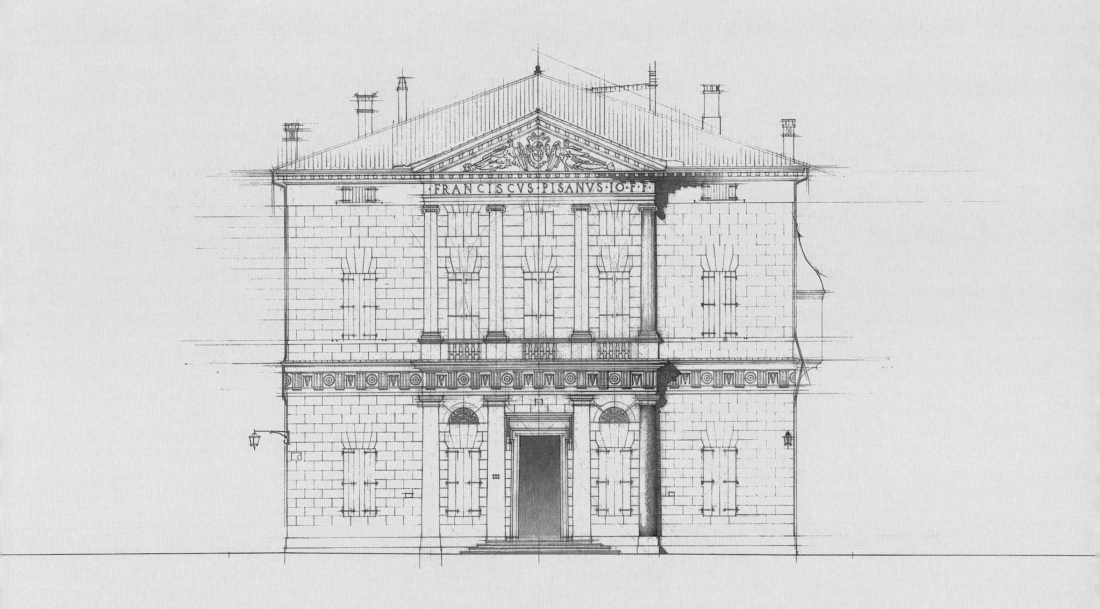

FRANCISCVS·PISANVS·IO·F·

75

VILLA CHIERICATI
(1554–1574)

In 1546, three brothers of the Chiericati family divided the family holdings between them. Two of the brothers became patrons of Palladio: Girolamo Chiericati commissioned Palladio to build the imposing Palazzo Chiericati in Vicenza, today the Museo Civico; and Giovanni Chiericati commissioned Palladio to build the Villa Chiericati. The villa is located along the road from Vicenza to Padua, in Vancimuglio, a *frazione* of the municipality of Grumolo delle Abbadesse in the province of Vicenza, and can be seen in passing from the autostrada A4. It was probably designed in the late 1540s, and was under construction by 1554. Although Palladio did not include the villa in his *Four Books*, a drawing by him of its plan is in the RIBA collection.[37] When Giovanni Chiericati died in 1558, the villa was still without a roof or colonnades. In 1574, the property was purchased by Ludovico Porto, who had the villa completed by 1584 by Domenico Groppino, a local architect.

Villa Chiericati is characterized by Palladio's usual tripartite division, but here the deep projecting loggia completely dominates the facade. This is Palladio's first use of a true temple front proceeding from the main body of the house, an element known in classical architecture as a *pronaos*; he was to use it with such success in later villas such as Villa Badoer, Villa Foscari (the "Malcontenta"), and Villa Almerico (the "Rotonda") that it has come to be identified with him. Although Villa Chiericati has only one *piano nobile*, it is exceptionally tall. A semibasement provided cool storage for fruits and other perishables, and a well-ventilated space under the eaves served as a granary. The loggia is screened by four towering Ionic columns *in antis*, which reach the full height of the living and granary floors together, thus forming a "colossal order," a colonnade that is more than one story

high. The colossal order is aptly proportioned here: the giant columns are crowned by a large pediment, whose details are very plastic; the dentils cast deep shadows, perfectly in scale with the great height of the loggia.

The plan of the villa is similar to that of Villa Cornaro. Its loggia opens to a narrow entry hall, which opens laterally to rectangular rooms on either side and to the square *salone* behind. Medium and small square rooms and stairwells are located on either side of the *salone*. There is no rear loggia, however, as at the Villa Cornaro, nor are the stairs given great importance, since they did not lead to a second *piano nobile* but were mainly for service. Palladio's plan for the villa shows a much more elaborate design for the *salone* than was actually built. He had planned a rectangular shape with apses at either end and cross vaults, but the built space has the simplicity of a cube, its ceiling beamed rather than vaulted. It is not known exactly when the design was changed, whether during Palladio's involvement, or in the second phase of the villa's construction under Groppino's supervision.

Symmetry is particularly important in the Villa Chiericati. The inner windows of the long rectangular rooms flanking the entry hall are aligned with the intercolumniations of the loggia; that is, they are located so that, looking out, one looks between the columns. Because the rectangular rooms are symmetrical, the windows must be located at equal distances from the room's corners. This means, however, that on the facade the outer windows are very close to the building's corners, a situation that Palladio discouraged in the *Four Books*.[38] Palladio was able to refine and correct this situation in the Villa Cornaro.

Today the villa is known as Chiericati da Porto Rigo and is privately owned. The gardens are open for visits every day, but the interiors are closed.

VILLA BARBARO

(1556–1558)

Villa Barbaro at Maser, some twenty-seven miles northwest of Vicenza in the province of Treviso, may well be Palladio's most unusual villa and was certainly built for unusual clients. Daniele and Marc'Antonio Barbaro, both learned humanists, were brothers, Venetian noblemen who were active in the politics of church and state. Palladio probably first met Daniele Barbaro when he accompanied Gian Giorgio Trissino to Padua in the late 1530s, in the early days of Palladio's architectural training. After the death of Trissino in 1550, Daniele and Marc'Antonio Barbaro became Palladio's most important benefactors and collaborators. They not only commissioned him to design—probably *with* them more than *for* them—the Villa Barbaro and the small chapel known as the Tempietto Barbaro adjacent to the villa, but helped him to obtain other important commissions as well, such as the facade of the church of San Francesco della Vigna and the church of Il Redentore, both in Venice. Daniele was an ecclesiastic, holding the title of Patriarch Elect of Aquileia. A scholar as well as a churchman, he published, in 1556, an important edition of Vitruvius's *Ten Books of Architecture*, for which Palladio furnished the illustrations. Undoubtedly, this collaboration was of fundamental importance to the development of Palladio's own *Four Books*. Marc'Antonio was just as formidable a figure. Active in the public affairs of the Venetian Republic, he nevertheless found time for architecture. Palladio credits him with the invention of a cantilevered staircase:

> Besides the usual types of stairs, the illustrious Signor Marc'Antonio Barbaro, a Venetian gentleman of great intellect, invented a spiral staircase that works very well in highly restricted locations. It does not have a column in the middle, and the steps, since they spiral, turn out to be very long.[39]

Marc'Antonio was an accomplished sculptor as well, and personally designed and executed much of the decoration for the Villa Barbaro.

The villa is situated on a long, sloping site, nestled at the foot of a ridge below the Dolomites, the Italian Alps. The dark evergreens on the ridge behind the villa provide a natural *scaenae frons*, or theatrical backdrop, against which the yellow and white facade of the villa shines forth. In front of the villa is an open vista to the vast, flat agricultural fields that seem to stretch without end. This is a villa complex more than a simple *casa dominicale*, similar in concept to the villa complexes of Villa Badoer and Villa Emo. There are several unusual elements in this design that set it apart from other villas of Palladio. Although the theme of the tripartite division is found in several aspects of the villa (the tripartite division of the principal facade by the colossal Ionic order, the central residential block flanked by symmetrical wings on either side, and the three-arched articulation of the end blocks), this is the only villa of Palladio's in which the central block is not divided into three parts. The principal residential block is clearly a single element topped by a pediment, whose tympanum, or triangular surface, is richly carved.

Behind the house, carved into the hillside is a semicircular *nymphaeum* built in 1565, a cool retreat with a fountain decorated "with an abundance of stucco and painted ornament,"[40] as Palladio wrote. The architrave rest on telamons and the raking cornice gently slopes to a peak in the center. A natural spring provides water to the *nymphaeum*; Palladio's attention to the integration of function and beauty is nowhere more apparent than in his own description of the use of the water:

> This fountain forms a little lake that serves as a fishpond; having left this spot, the water runs to the kitchen and then, having irrigated the gardens to right and left of the road which gently ascends and leads to the building, forms two fishponds with their horse troughs on the public road; from there it goes off to water the orchard.[41]

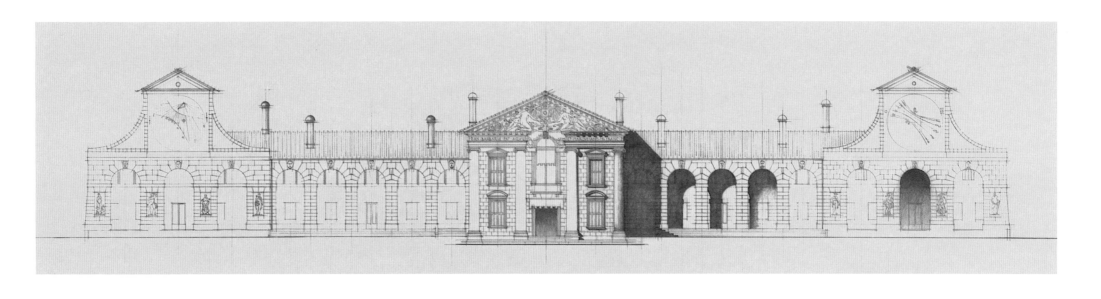

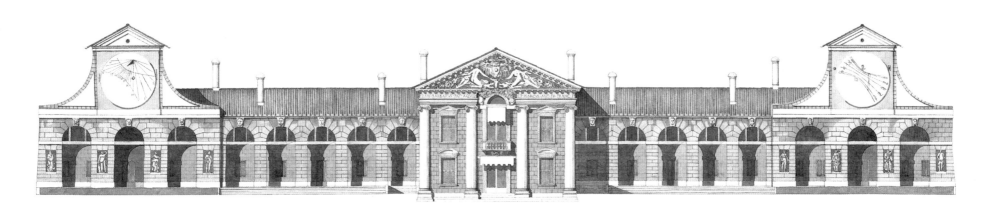

Due to the sloping site, the *piano nobile* is on the same level as the *nymphaeum* at the rear, but is fully one story above ground at the front, providing a splendid view of the property from the cross-vaulted *salone*. The symmetrical loggias on either side are, as befits farm buildings, much simpler and less decorated than the *casa dominicale*. The main decorations on the end buildings are very large sundials, which are functional as well as ornamental. The scrolls that form the visual transition between the lower floors and the dovecots of the end buildings are unusual in Palladio's work. He indicated smaller but similar scrolls for the facade of the Villa Foscari, but these were not built.

It is the explicit references to classical and contemporary interpretations of classical architecture that most distinguish Villa Barbaro from Palladio's other villas. Where Palladio usually abstracted classical elements and reelaborated them in his own style, here we find elements that are almost copies: the Ionic columns of the facade take after those of the Temple of Fortuna Virilius in Rome; the *nymphaeum* takes after that of Vignola for the Villa Giulia in Rome; the balconies of the *casa dominicale* take after those of Michelangelo for St. Peter's. This more than anything else may indicate that Palladio worked closely with his patrons to realize their concept rather than his own.

The villa as built differs only in its details from Palladio's woodcut in the *Four Books*. On the main facade, for instance, he has broken the horizontal cornice of the pediment so that the arched opening can reach up to the top of the barrel vault in the *salone*; and the upper stories of the outer wings of the *barchesse* have been raised where round sundials fit in place of the oval niches indicated in the woodcut.

The frescoes inside the villa are the excellent work of Paolo Veronese, and while they work very well with the spaces of the villa, they illustrate an architecture that is very different from the kind that Palladio designed. Palladio did not credit Veronese in the *Four Books*, leading scholars to question whether he approved of the frescoes, but it seems likely that he left the artistic decoration up to the artists and the patrons. Today the Villa Barbaro is privately owned and open for visits.

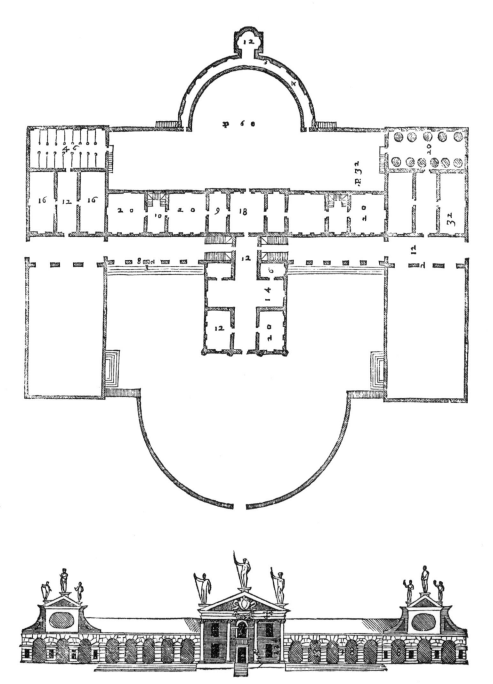

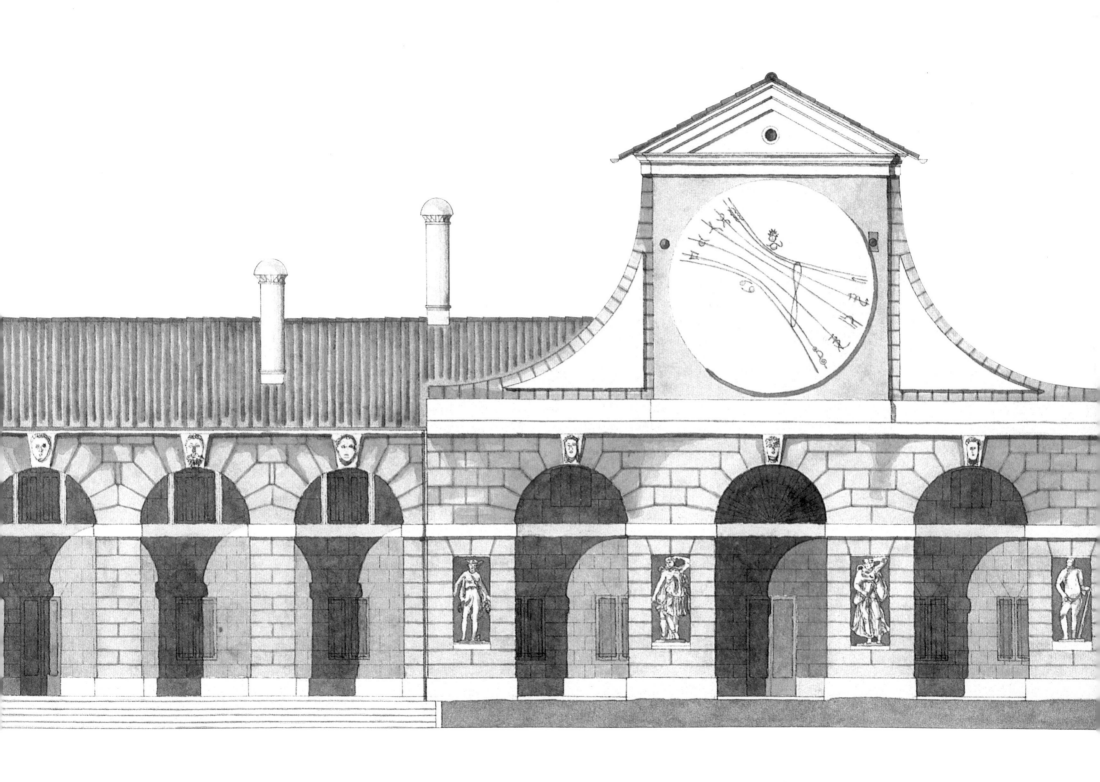

VILLA BADOER
(1556–1563)

Villa Badoer was commissioned by Francesco Badoer, a powerful Venetian nobleman. His wife, Lucietta, was a member of the Loredan family, who could count doges of Venice among their number. Upon his brother-in-law's death, Badoer had obtained property in Fratta Polesine, in the province of Rovigo, at the farthest confines of the Venetian *terraferma* territory. Work on his villa took place within the second half of the 1550s.

The villa's main facade faced onto a tributary of the Adige River. Today a bridge over this waterway links the villa to the main street through the town. A levee has been built to protect from flooding, so the villa is a few steps lower than the street. The villa complex is completely enclosed, by buildings on the two front sides and by walls elsewhere. The vast expanses of flat fields that are characteristic of the Veneto can only be seen through the gate in the back.

Villa Badoer was built atop the foundations of an earlier medieval castle, a brick basement of which is still visible at the villa's rear today; Palladio took advantage of this existing structure to give the villa extra height. The complex is indeed imposing, made the more so by the monumental two-flight staircase leading up to the loggia, and the curving *barchesse* on either side connecting to the linear buildings that line the building's forecourt. While we today think of a villa as a house, it was really this whole complex of buildings that Palladio had in mind when he used the term "villa," with the main house, or *casa dominicale*, at its center. The *barchesse*, whose function Palladio described as serving for storage of farm equipment and even animals, in actuality principally served to keep the villa's *padrone* dry as he went about his business supervising the farm. Villa Badoer's *barchesse*, however, are not well integrated with the main house, since they are situated much lower than it, due to its high basement. They are reached by flights of stairs that intersect the main stair laterally at the intermediate landing. The relationship of house to *barchesse* is much better resolved at Villa Barbaro and Villa Emo. The structure of the *barchesse* themselves, however, is very graceful, with smooth, curving brick walls and Tuscan columns supporting simple wooden, triangular trusses. Palladio's use of the rustic Tuscan order for the agricultural wings contrasts with his use of the Ionic order for the loggia, emphasizing the exalted status of the latter.

The tripartite composition of the plan allows us to see clearly how Palladio exploited this kind of division of the building's mass for structural purposes: load-bearing walls run from the foundations to the rafters back to front through the house in line with the loggia and the *salone*. The front loggia opens to long rectangular rooms at its sides and to the long, narrow *salone* behind. Square rooms are in each of the back corners. The *salone* is flanked by small rectangular spaces, two to a side with stairs placed in the two front rooms, while the back spaces are frescoed *studioli*, little studies. As the woodcut in the *Four Books* shows, Palladio had also planned a back loggia, but this was never built.

The villa today is owned by the province of Rovigo and is closed for restoration. The fragments of frescoes by Giallo Fiorentino are in sad repair.

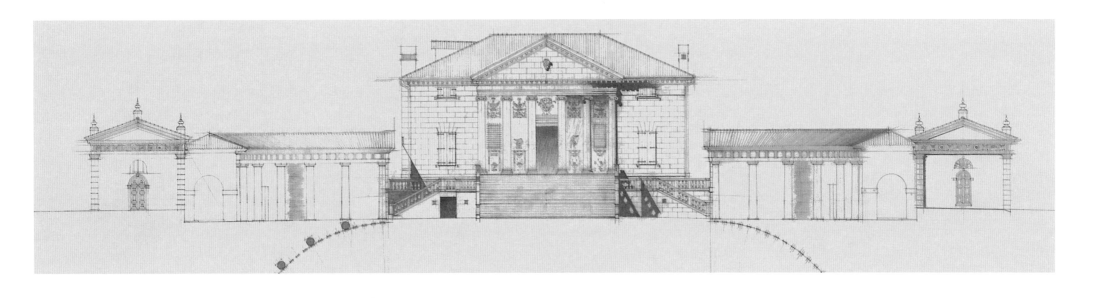

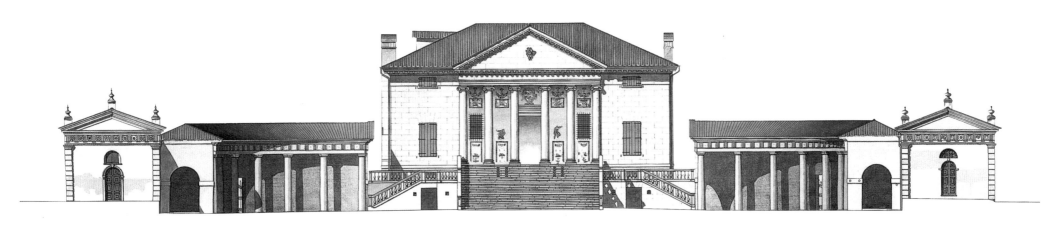

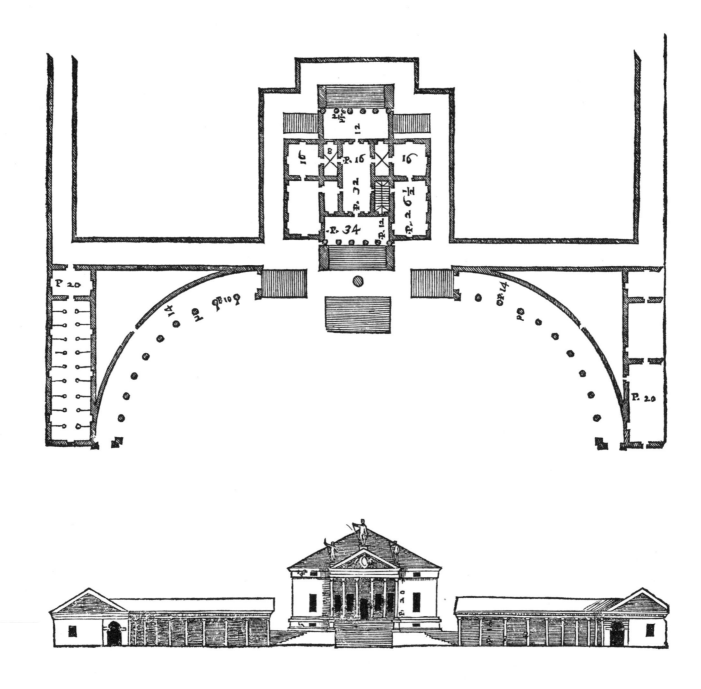

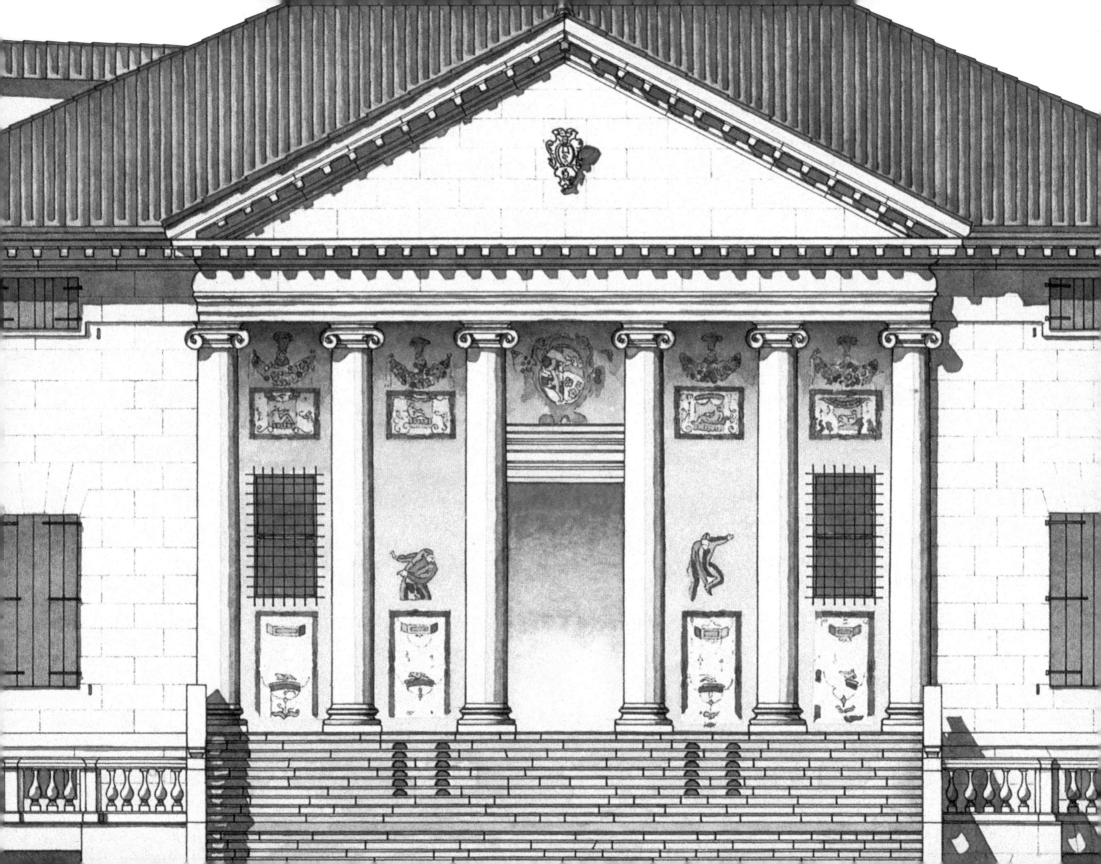

VILLA THIENE, CICOGNA
(1556–1563)

The Thiene family was the wealthiest family of Vicenza, proprietors of expensive property in the city and expansive estates in the surrounding countryside. One of Palladio's first contacts with the family was through Marco Thiene, a poet who traveled with Trissino and Palladio to Rome; he was a distant cousin of Marc'Antonio and Adriano Thiene and the nephew of Francesco Thiene. The palace for Marc'Antonio and Adriano, the Palazzo Thiene on the Contrà Porti, was one of Palladio's greatest early opportunities to prove himself. Marc'Antonio and Adriano also commissioned Palladio to design their villa at Quinto. Villa Thiene at Cicogna was designed for Francesco Thiene, who also commissioned Palladio to design his palace in the Piazza Castello in Vicenza, and his sons, counts Odoardo and Theodoro Thiene. Francesco's wife, Isabella, was the sister of Alessandro Porto, who commissioned the Palazzo Porto Breganze, the colossal two finished bays of which are situated on the other side of the same piazza. Theodoro Thiene, Francesco's son, married Diamante Pepoli, whose brother obtained the commission for Palladio to design the new facade for Bologna's San Petronio cathedral, never realized. Other relatives of the Thienes commissioned works by Palladio as well, such as the Palazzo Porto in Vicenza and the Palazzo Barbarano in Vicenza. It can be seen by this web of relationships how Palladio's reputation grew through his association with the Thienes, and how important their patronage was for him.

In 1539, Francesco's branch of the Thiene family had acquired property in Cicogna, a *frazione* of Villafranca Padovana in the province of Padua. By the mid-1550s, when Francesco commissioned Palladio to design his villa, there already existed a house with several outbuildings on their property. Palladio's task was to reorganize the site, including a new disposition of roads, and to design a new villa complex with the *casa dominicale* and *barchesse*. Although work was begun on the project, it was soon interrupted by the death of Francesco in 1556. It continued under Odoardo and Theodoro, but when Odoardo, accused of heresy by the Inquisition, went into exile to the Protestant community of Geneva in 1567, construction was halted and was never resumed. The new roads and a single *barchessa* are all that remain.

The *barchessa* that we see today features a fine arcade articulated by applied Tuscan pilasters. Similar arcaded *barchesse*, providing a more enclosed space than colonnaded wings, are found at Villa Barbaro and Villa Emo. The end of the *barchessa* opens through an arch with mannerist voussoirs. This end arch was to have opened onto colonnaded *barchesse* in the form of hemicycles, such as those at Villa Badoer. The woodcut in the *Four Books* shows the *casa dominicale* with two *piani nobili* and a central loggia with a colossal Corinthian order. The loggia was to have been flanked by flat-roofed, intermediate blocks and towers on the corners. Palladio used a variation of this idea in his design for the Villa Valmarana at Lisiera.

As always, the site of the villa was as important to Palladio as the design of the villa itself. He was particularly pleased with the new roads laid out for Villa Thiene, which were lined with trees on either side:

> And just as in cities the beauty of roads is increased by the addition of beautiful buildings, so outside the cities their attractiveness is increased by trees, which, when planted on either side of them, cheer us up with their greenness and make them extremely comfortable with the shade they provide. There are many roads of this type in the Vicentino, and amongst them are the famous ones at Cicogna, the estate of Count Odoardo Thiene, and at Quinto, the estate of signor the Count Ottavio of the same family, devised by me, which were then improved and embellished by the care and industry of those gentlemen.[42]

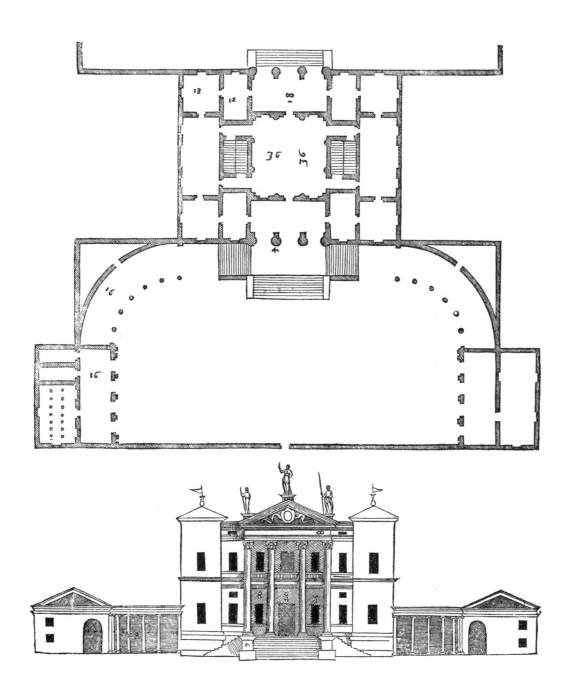

VILLA REPETA
(1557–1558)

Villa Repeta was built for Palladio's most colorful patrons. A Vicentine noble family, the Repetas had held their estate in Campiglia, south of Vicenza in the Berici hills, since the early thirteenth century. In the mid-1550s, Francesco Repeta commissioned Palladio to design a new villa for the estate. Francesco died in 1556, but his son Mario took over in his father's place and finished the construction.

Palladio planned the villa as a courtyard building without a central "villa" house, an idea that he would later develop in the Villa Sarego in Santa Sofia. As shown in the *Four Books*, the residence was formed by three *barchessa*-like porticoes in a U-shape, with an enclosing wall on the fourth side of the courtyard. Towers with gaily flying flags mark the corners of the courtyard, and a pediment with three statues on acroteria signal the principal entrance to the villa.

Vasari was impressed by the arrangement and luxury of the Villa Repeta: "At Campiglia, in the Vicentine, he [Palladio] made…a residence with many conveniences, rich apartments of rooms, loggias, courtyards and rooms dedicated to various virtues…more fit for a king than for a lord."[43] The "virtues" to whom Vasari refers are the subjects of the frescoes in the various rooms, such as Continence and Justice. As Palladio wrote, Mario Repeta could "accommodate his visitors and friends in the room of the Virtue to which their dispositions appear to him most inclined."[44] The frescoes were painted by Giambattista Maganza, who was also a protégé of Gian Giorgio Trissino, and who had accompanied Trissino and Palladio to Rome to study the latest architecture and painting of the capital.

Villa Repeta as we see it today is very different from the unusual structure originally designed by Palladio, but reflects many of the principles set forth in Palladio's other villas. The facade is divided into three parts, with the central part projecting slightly forward and crowned by a triangular pediment, carved with the Repeta coat of arms. The entrance to the loggia is articulated by three arches with exaggerated voussoirs and an applied classical order. The architrave of the lower floor is carried around the villa as a continuous string molding, uniting the three parts of the villa.

One curious feature of the villa that remains are the prominent obelisks that sit atop the side portions. These were a sign that there was a high-ranking officer of the navy, such as an admiral, in the family. (Compare these very large obelisks with similar, smaller ones that appear on either side of the entrance loggia at Villa Cornaro.) Today the Villa Repeta-Bressan is privately owned and can be visited by appointment.

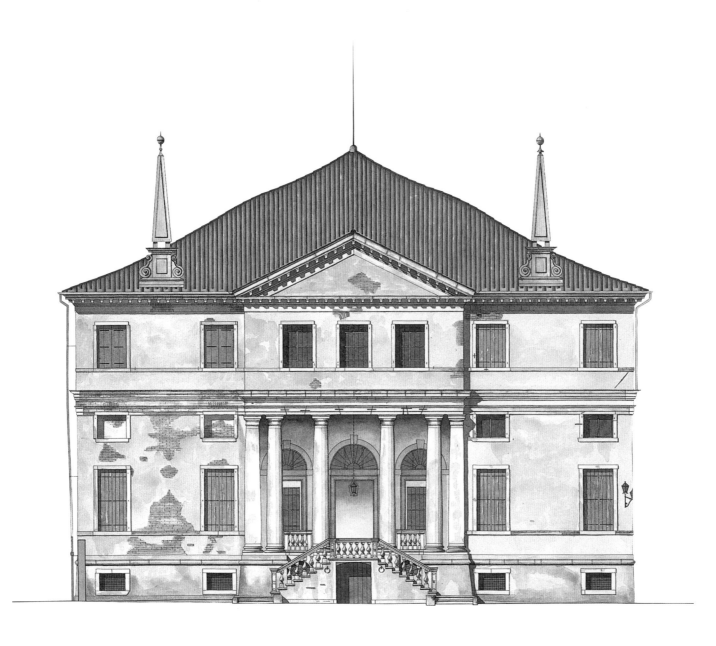

93

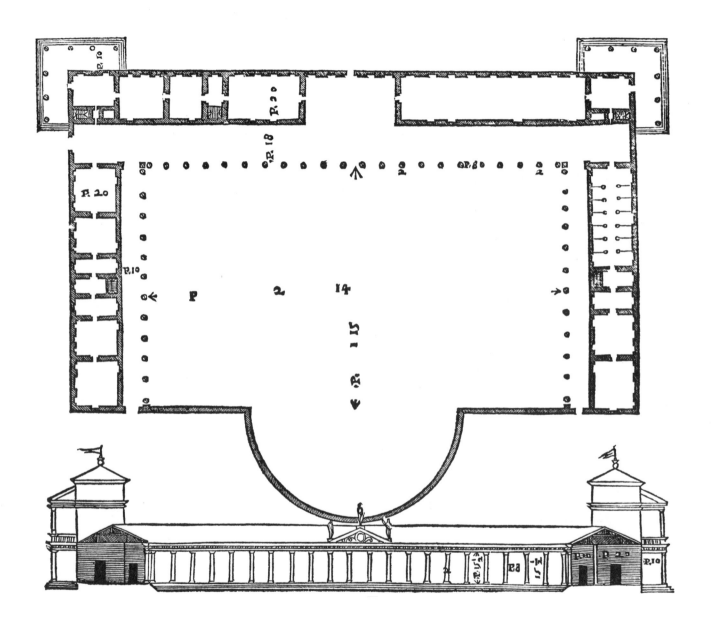

94

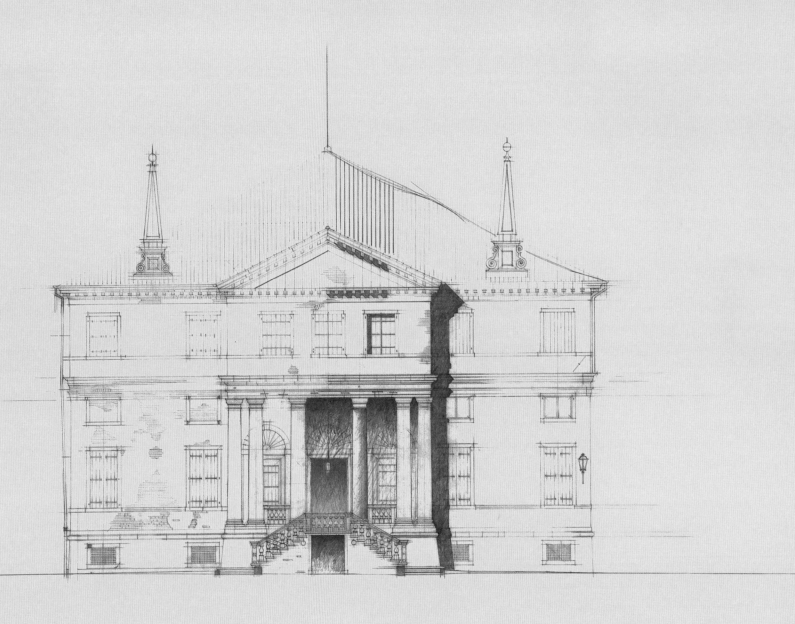

95

VILLA FOSCARI, THE "MALCONTENTA"
(1558–1561)

Members of one of Venice's most powerful families, brothers Nicolò and Luigi Foscari, commissioned Palladio to design a villa in the late 1550s. The villa was built on the Brenta Canal in Malcontenta, a *frazione* of Mira, just a short boat trip away from Venice. Like Villa Cornaro and Villa Pisani at Montagnana, Villa Foscari is a hybrid between villa and palace, but this is the first instance in which the villa had no relation to a functioning farm. Villa Foscari was intended to be the patrons' noble country residence as well as a clear sign of their status. The brothers spared no expense for the villa, and Palladio was able for the first time to design on a truly grand scale.

The property faced the Brenta Canal, an important waterway in and out of the Venetian lagoon, and Palladio was able to use this natural feature of the site to the advantage of the architecture. Facing the canal, the colossal Ionic order and triangular pediment of the majestic loggia send a clear message about the status of the owners. The image of majesty is further heightened by the full-story basement on which the loggia sits. The high water table of the site made it impossible to create a semibasement as was usual in the villas, but Palladio turned this defect into a virtue by using the service floor as a dais upon which to place the loggia. The brick belt at the bottom of the ground floor lends an air of strength and solidity. Grand right-angled stairs on either side of the loggia bring visitors to the *piano nobile*. The *intonaco* of the facade is deeply raked to resemble stone coursing, adding relief to the flat surfaces, especially on the garden facade. Villa Foscari's garden facade is typical of the Palladian vocabulary, articulated into three parts, with the central part projecting slightly. The broken pediment is similar to that of Villa Poiana, but its application here is more

logical, because the thermal window placed in the end of the *salone*'s vault arches up beyond the height of the horizontal cornice of the pediment.

Similar to the Villa Thiene in Quinto, which was also planned for two brothers, the plan of Villa Foscari provides separate, symmetrical apartments on either side of the common loggia and *salone*. The plan of the villa is similar to that of Villa Pisani at Bagnolo, but the transfer of the stairs from the middle of the villa to its rear results in the cruciform *salone*, which is vaulted with a hybrid cross and barrel vault. The frescoes on the vaults were executed by Battista Franco and Giambattista Zelotti.

Tradition has it that the villa's nickname, "Malcontenta," dates to the eighteenth century, when an unhappy woman of the Foscari family, believed to have betrayed her husband, was exiled there. The village of Malcontenta was supposedly given its name in the 1430s to express discontent over Venice's decree that the Brenta be diverted through it. In spite of the name, many happy and auspicious occasions took place in the villa, such as the visit of French king Henry III in 1574 and that of the king of Denmark and Norway in 1709. But there were sad events in the villa's life as well: patron Nicolò Foscari died in 1560, just as the villa was finished, and painter Battista Franco died in 1561, while he was frescoing the *salone*. Perhaps the saddest event of all was the occupation of the villa by Austrian soldiers in the mid-nineteenth century, which resulted in the destruction of the *barchesse* and the surrounding park of trees. Only good fortune rescued the frescoes at the last moment, when one of the later owners of the villa had contracted to remove and sell them. In recent years the villa has fared better. It now belongs once again to the Foscari family, and has been carefully restored. The villa is open for visits.

NICOLAVS ET ALOYSIVS FOSCARI FRATRES FEDERICI FILII

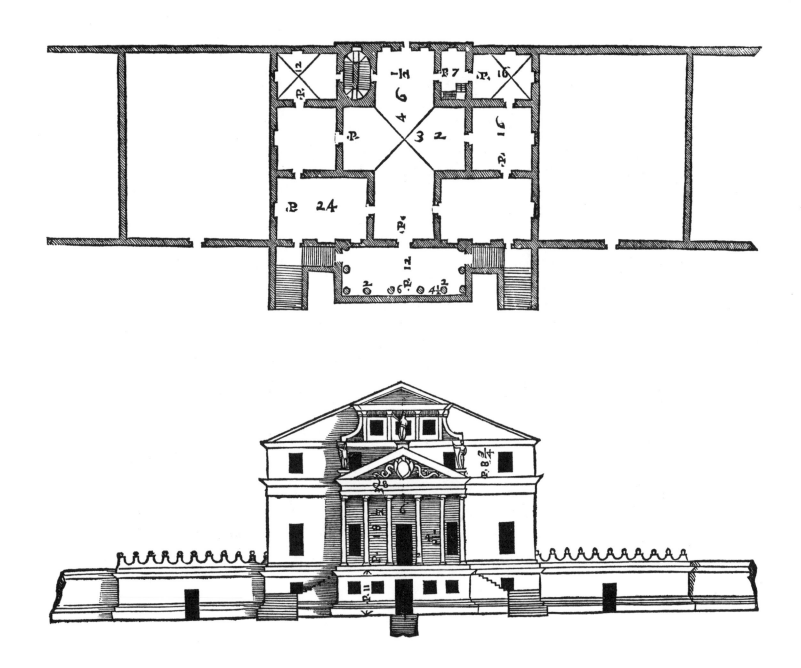

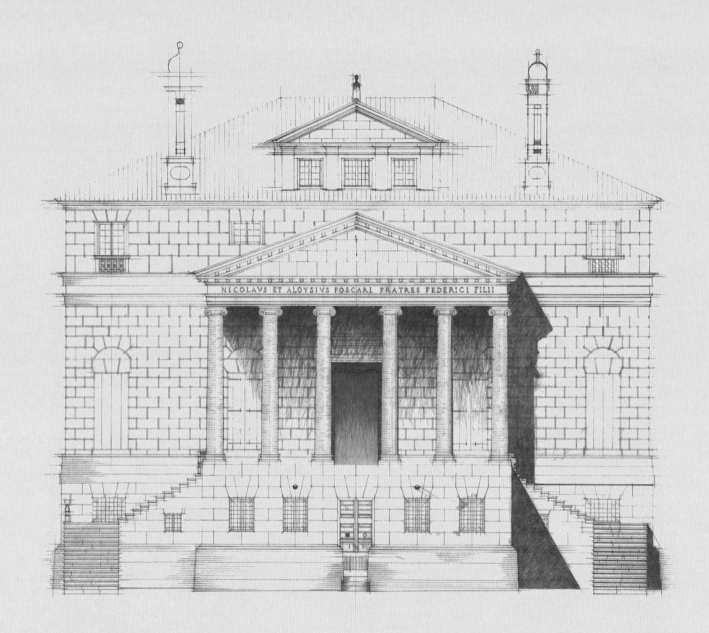

NICOLAVS ET ALOYSIVS FOSCARI FRATRES FEDERICI FILII

VILLA TRISSINO, MELEDO

(1558–1562)

By the mid-1550s, Palladio had reached his full maturity as a villa designer. Not only had he made a vocabulary of classical elements his own but he had mastered the use of a grand scale as a means of expression. This becomes evident if we compare a smaller, earlier villa such as Villa Gazzotti, which is clearly domestic architecture in spite of the use of an applied classical order and a pedimented front, with a later, grander villa such as Villa Foscari, in which the colossal Ionic order of the loggia takes the building out of the genre of domestic architecture and into the realm of the monumental. Palladio's scheme for the Villa Trissino at Meledo, a *frazione* of Sarego in the province of Vicenza, was designed to be most monumental. The villa was commissioned by brothers, the counts Francesco and Ludovico Trissino. Francesco and Ludovico were of a different branch of the family of Gian Giorgio Trissino, Palladio's early mentor, and were important patrons of Palladio's. Ludovico had backed the selection of Palladio as the architect for the Basilica in Vicenza in 1549. In addition to the villa, they also commissioned him to design a palace on their property on the Contrà Riale in Vicenza. Unfortunately, neither project was ever realized, but a single *barchessa* and foundations indicate that the Villa Trissino was at least begun.

As he so often did, Palladio took his inspiration for the design from the natural features of the site, describing the location enthusiastically in the *Four Books*: "The site is stunning, since it is on a hill which is bathed by a pleasant little river; it is in the middle of a great plain and to one side is a busy road."[45] The hill gave Palladio the very opportunity he needed to design a true free-standing temple set within a larger complex of subordinate buildings. He modeled his design on the Roman temple complex at Palestrina. A drawing of Palladio's in the RIBA collection[46] shows a centrally planned temple with identical loggias on all sides and a low dome with a lantern, such as the villa that he depicts in the *Four Books*.

What can be seen today in Meledo is an entrance gate and the loggia of a *barchessa* attached to what was probably an existing building with a dovecot tower. Palladio preferred the Tuscan order for the *barchesse*, in part because the Tuscan order was the least refined of the orders; as he writes, "The Tuscan order is the most plain and simple of all the orders of architecture, for it retains an air of primitive antiquity about it and lacks all those ornaments which make the other orders admirable and beautiful."[47] In spite of their humble nature, the workmanship on the Tuscan columns here is very fine, an indication that no expense would have been spared in the construction of the villa.

Villa Trissino was not completed, but fortunately Palladio was able to reuse its central idea for the Villa Almerico. The great opportunity that was missed was that of building an entire villa complex in which site and architecture combined to produce a hierarchical grouping of buildings. The fragments that are visible today are tantalizing allusions to the grandeur that might have been.

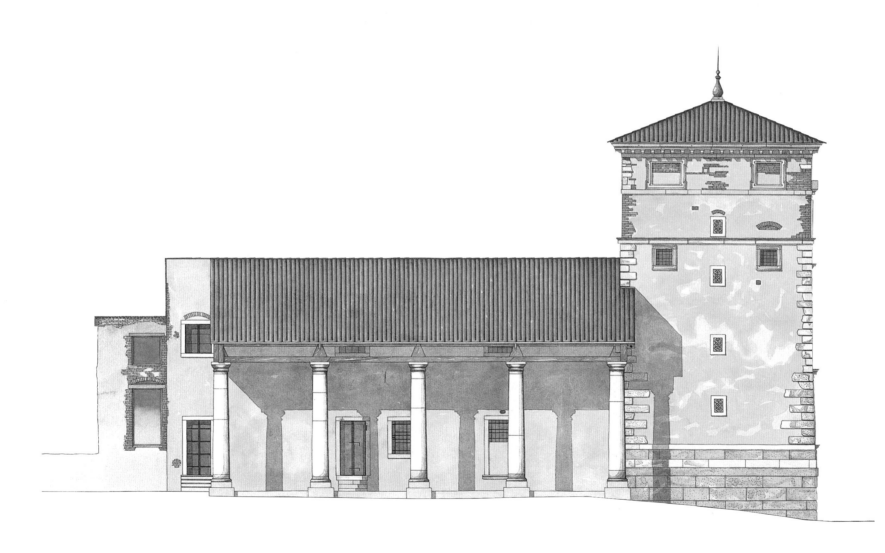

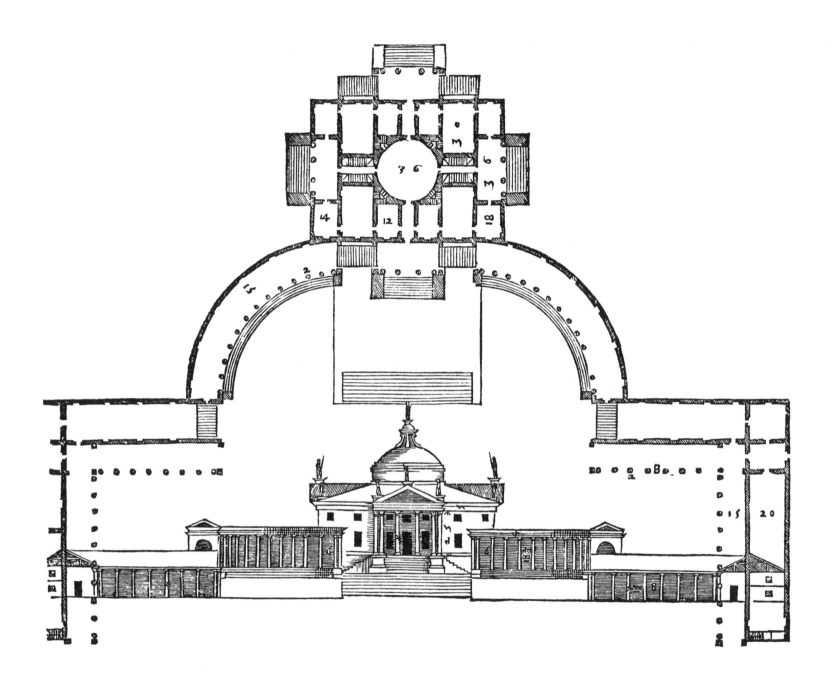

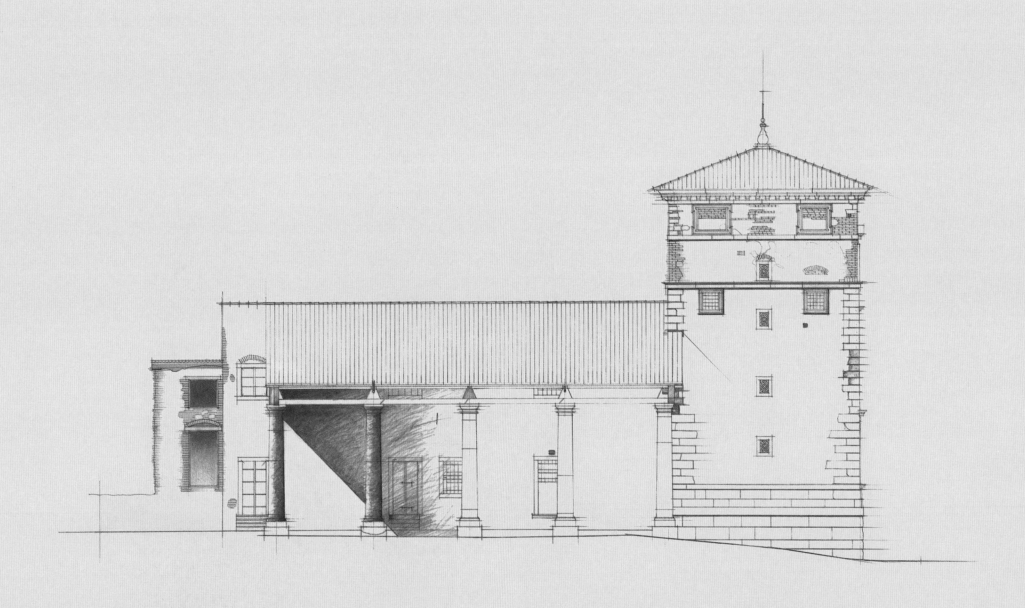

103

VILLA ZENO

(1558–1566?)

"The magnificent Signor Marco Zeno"[48] was a powerful political figure in Venice and had been *podestà*, or mayor, of that city in 1558–1559. He owned a large estate in Cessalto, of 450 *campi* (about 450 acres), and commissioned Palladio to build his villa there. The date of construction is uncertain. The styles of its courtyard and garden facades link it to early villas, but documents indicate that the date may be as late as the mid-1560s. It is one of the villas about which the least is known, and is the one that deviates the most from Palladio's design for it in the *Four Books*. In its dilapidated state, it is also one of the saddest.

Villa Zeno's courtyard facade is devoid of any division into parts, except for what is intimated by the pediment that floats over the center of the facade. As planned by Palladio, the courtyard facade was to have had a thermal window, one of Palladio's favorite motives, which appears on the garden facades of Villa Godi, Villa Pisani at Bagnolo, and Villa Foscari. Had it been built, it would have illuminated and outlined the barrel vault of the *salone*, and added considerable interest to the facade; but it was not built, and it is unknown whether the change was made with Palladio's approval or after he was no longer involved with the villa. The *salone* is flanked by large rectangular rooms with fireplaces in the middle of their long, exterior walls. This presents the same problem with which Palladio grappled at Villa Godi and resolved in Villa Gazzotti—windows symmetrically located on either side of the fireplace are then very close to the villa's outer corners, a situation Palladio warned against. It appears that Palladio had to accommodate an existing structure as part of his design, and thus might not have been able to control this. The courtyard on which the villa opens should have been defined by U-shaped, colonnaded *barchesse* but again these were unrealized. The existing agricultural wings were constructed in the seventeenth and eighteenth centuries. The fact that the villa was a functioning farm may explain its essential and unadorned architecture.

The villa's garden facade is dominated by a recessed loggia screened by three simple arches, rather like that of Villa Saraceno in Finale. Here, however, no stair leads to the loggia, as it is at ground level; its arches are consequently extraordinarily tall. As on the courtyard facade, a pediment floats over the garden facade's central portion.

Villa Zeno is located far from any of Palladio's other works, in Cessalto, north of the town of Ceggia on the provincial road that runs between Treviso and Motta di Livenza. Today it is not lived in, and is in a state of ruin. The exterior, inside a courtyard, can always be seen, but the interior cannot be visited.

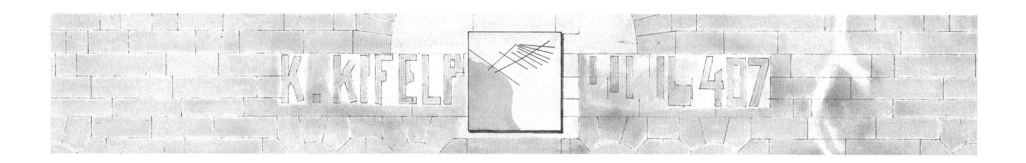

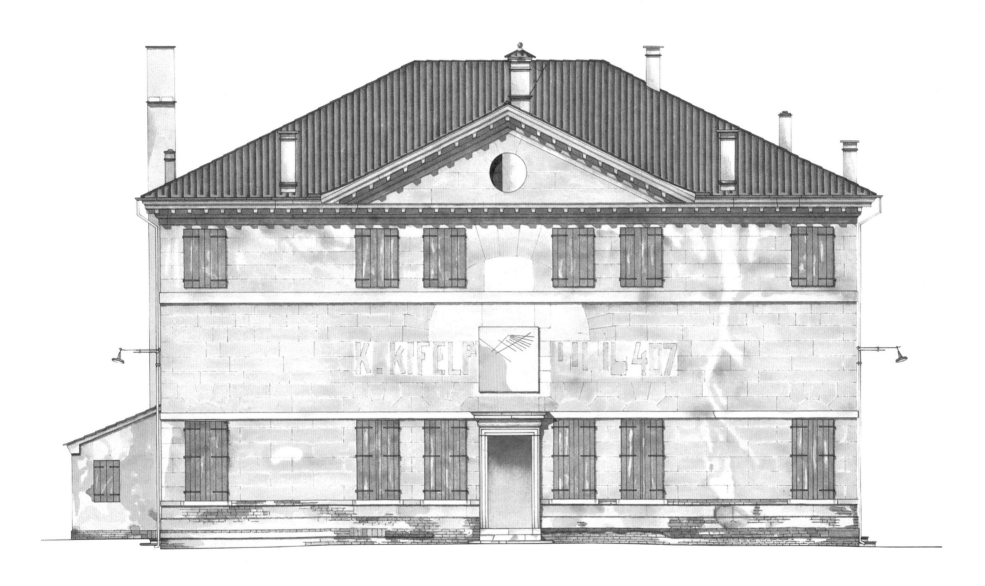

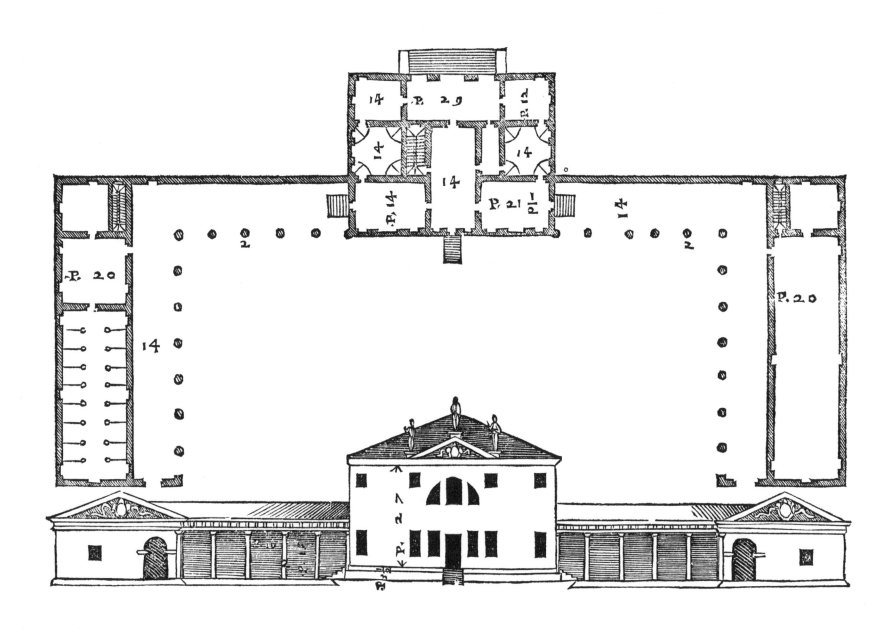

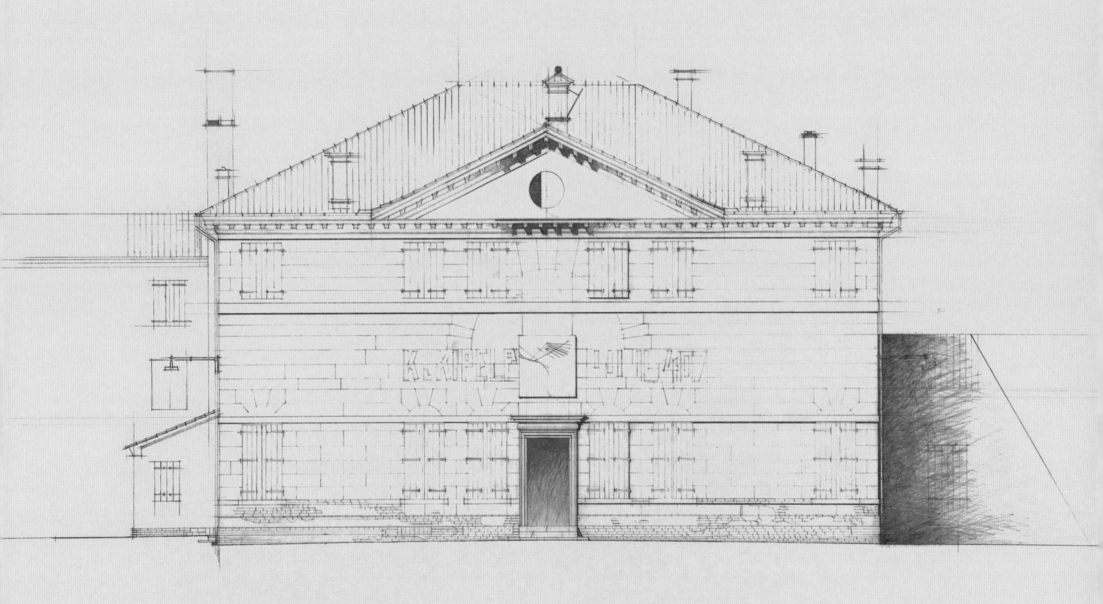

VILLA EMO
(1560–1565)

Villa Emo at Fanzolo, a *frazione* of Vedelago in the province of Treviso, is a planning masterpiece of Palladio's mature villas, combining abstracted classical elements with a functioning farm. The 250-acre estate of the Emos, bought in 1509, was almost entirely swampland, which was subsequently reclaimed. Leonardo Emo, a great innovator, was the first to begin cultivating maize, at that time newly imported from the New World and today a mainstay of Venetan agriculture. Leonardo's gamble with the new crop paid off, for it increased the property's income fivefold. At the end of the 1550s, Emo commissioned Palladio to design a villa to embody his vision of a country residence that was functional as well as formal, and that recognized a social hierarchy of proprietor, farmers and peasants, and craftsmen and artists. Palladio's design responds by setting out a *casa dominicale* flanked by symmetrical, linear *barchesse*, and situating this composition so that it faces the group of peasants' houses across the villa's expansive forecourt. The peasants' houses still exist today, conveying a sense of the villa as a true, hierarchical complex.

The *casa dominicale* is composed of a semibasement and *piano nobile*, which is reached by a monumental ramp. The ramp was functional as well as formal, since it could be used as a threshing and drying floor during the harvest. It has been speculated that the ramp allowed visitors to reach the loggia on horseback, but the present owner of the villa flatly refutes that, arguing that the way the ramp is divided into sections by raised strips would quickly lame a horse. The facade of the villa, surprisingly unornamented for its late date in Palladio's career, is divided into three parts. The central pavilion is given over to a recessed loggia with four Tuscan columns *in antis* crowned by a pediment, whose tympanum contains a sculpture of the Emo coat of arms held by a pair of reclining, winged figures. The loggia opens to a narrow entrance hall at

its rear, which in its turn leads to the square *salone*. The side portions are divided into suites of three rectangular and square rooms. The villa's famous frescoes, exceptionally well preserved, were executed by Giambattista Zelotti in 1565. In the room dedicated to the Arts, the allegorical figure for architecture holds a book that is open to the plan of the Villa Emo, her finger pointing to precisely the spot where the visitor is standing.

The arcaded *barchesse* with dovecots at both ends are completely unornamented except for the imposts of the arches, which provide visual horizontal continuity. Originally serving as work spaces and storage for farm equipment, they were adapted for residential use in the eighteenth century. The linear form of the *barchesse* here is similar to those of the Villa Barbaro and seems to have been influenced by a tradition that belonged to the Treviso area, as it appears in pre-Palladian villas of that area but not in any of Palladio's villas in other regions.

Scholars have spent much time discussing the proportions of Palladio's room sizes, and the Villa Emo is a very good example of how proportion was used in design. Palladio provides measurements in Vicentine feet (one Vicentine foot equals about 26 inches) for the various rooms, showing the *salone* as a 27 × 27 square, the larger rectangular rooms as 16 × 27, smaller rectangular rooms as 12 × 16, the small square rooms as 16 × 16, and the loggia as 16 × 27. In the *barchesse*, the room sizes are 12 × 20, 24 × 20, and 48 × 20. The numbers 12, 16, 24, 27, and 48 can be interpreted as belonging to a system of musical harmonies. In the fifteenth century, architect Leon Battista Alberti, author of the famous *Ten Books of Architecture*, by which Palladio was greatly influenced, had discussed these kinds of number relationships in terms of room sizes, and while Palladio was not dogmatic about their application, he certainly took them into

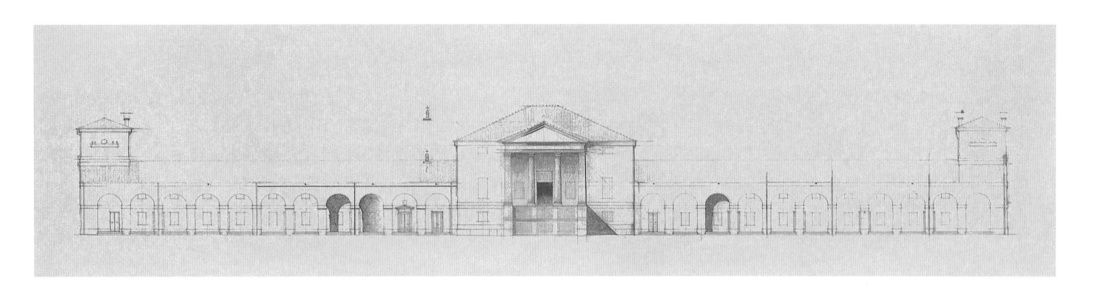

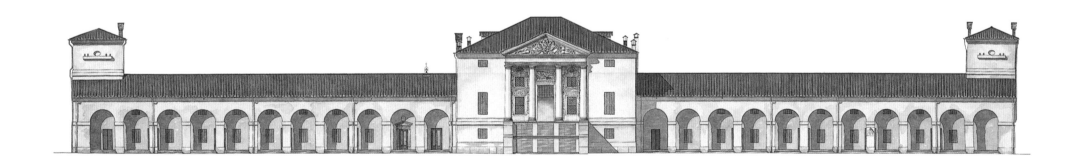

109

consideration when he was able to. Thus the 16 × 27 rectangular room can be interpreted as the extremes of the progression 16:24:27, translating musically into the intervals of a fifth (16:24 or 2:3) and a major whole tone (24:27 or 8:9). What is significant about the relationship between number and architecture is that it allowed individual elements to be integrated into a "harmonic" unity.

Today the villa is still the property of the Emo family, as it has been for eighteen continuous generations. The present Count Emo tried unsuccessfully to adapt the villa as a hotel and restaurant to make it self-sustaining but was blocked by bureaucratic restrictions on the use of properties that are historically significant. It has been on and off the market in recent years, but has not yet left the Emo family. The villa is open for visits.

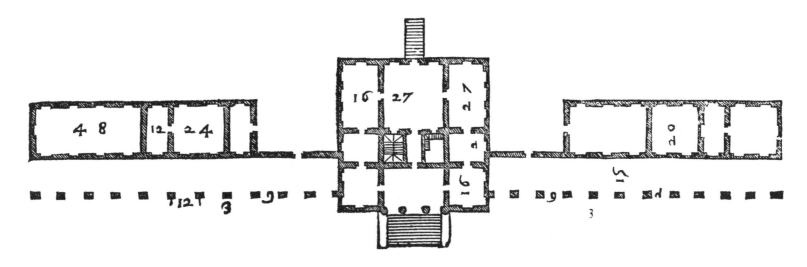

VILLA VALMARANA, LISIERA
(1563–1564)

Villa Valmarana in Lisiera, a *frazione* of Bolzano Vicentino, about three miles northeast of Vicenza, was designed by Palladio in about 1563 for Gianfrancesco Valmarana. Gianfrancesco was the brother of Giovanni Alvise Valmarana, who some years earlier, in the late 1550s, had commissioned Palladio to design the Palazzo Valmarana on Vicenza's Corso Fogazzaro. Although Gianfrancesco must have been impressed with Palladio's architectural skills, he initially engaged him to build a wooden bridge over the Tesina River, a sign of his confidence in Palladio as an engineer as well as an architect; the commission for the villa was probably given at the same time as that of the bridge.

Palladio's design as published in the *Four Books* shows a two-story loggia with a pediment, the kind of temple front that he designed for Villa Cornaro and Villa Pisani at Montagnana a decade earlier. Here he mixes this element of his mature villas with corner towers that hark back to the kind of castle-villas that were typical of the *terraferma* before Palladio began his career. The towers of Villa Valmarana particularly impressed Giorgio Vasari, who described the villa as "a very rich edifice with four towers at the corners, which are most beautiful to see."[49] Palladio was familiar with this kind of tower from his formative years in the Villa Trissino at Cricoli, and used them himself on the entrance facade of the Villa Pisani at Bagnolo. Between the square rooms in the towers and the loggias are located the four

stairwells, which were given a prominent location to emphasize the prestige of a house with two *piani nobili*. The facade of the villa is a departure from Palladio's usual tripartite division, since the stairs and corner towers appear as distinct elements on the facade. The plan too is different from his usual composition, lacking the clear hierarchy of a *salone* flanked by large, medium, and small rooms.

Construction began on the villa only to be brought to a halt in 1566 by the death of Gianfrancesco. His nephew, Leonardo, son of Giovanni Alvise, inherited the villa. Work undertaken in 1579–80 may have caused the villa to be finished as expediently as possible, truncating the upper floor, unifying the roofline, and simplifying the massing. It is unknown exactly when it assumed its final form, which features a kind of attic resting on the lower loggia and a simple roof minimizing the separate identities of the stairwells and corner towers. Over the centuries, various embellishments were made, including the addition of a chapel by Francesco Muttoni in 1615, carved stone balusters in the upper story windows later in the seventeenth century, and a formal garden and statues by Francesco Marinali in the eighteenth century. The worst blow of all for the villa came in World War II, when it was almost completely destroyed by bombing. It was restored in 1969 and is today privately owned. The exterior is visible from the road.

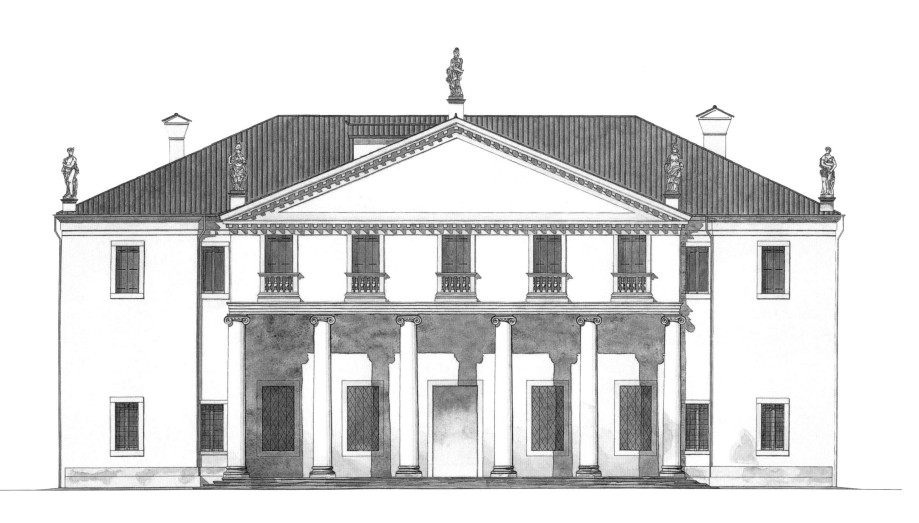

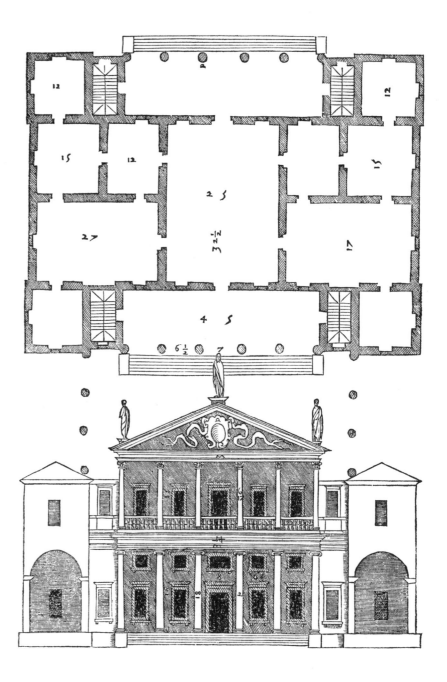

VILLA FORNI
(1560s)

Located north of Vicenza in Montecchio Precalcino, Villa Forni, spare, compact, and without *barchesse*, is similar in style to the villas designed by Palladio in the early 1540s at the beginning of his career; but documents appear to establish that it was designed in the 1560s. The austerity of the design, devoid of an architectural order, may have suited the commissioner, Girolamo Forni, who is unique among the villa owners in that he was not a member of the nobility. (The only other patron who was not born into nobility was Taddeo Gazzotti of the Villa Gazzotti, but he married into the aristocracy.) Forni was a very wealthy lumber merchant, a painter and collector of antiquities, and, like Palladio, a member of Vicenza's Olympic Academy. Palladio was commissioned to restructure an existing house, which may explain why this design seems so lacking in his usual attention to proportion.

Villa Forni presents the usual tripartite facade, with a central body that projects beyond the flanking wings. The villa shows a more plastic treatment of the central element, however, than the other villas designed with this spare aesthetic, where a mere impression of projection is given by a very shallow shadow line. To tie the central body and the wings together into a single composition in spite of the deep projection of the central element, Palladio uses the device of a continuous string molding.

Villa Forni has a semibasement for kitchen and service spaces, a single *piano nobile* for living spaces, and an upper floor that could be used for living or for service as the need presented itself. The entrance to Villa Forni is in the form of a *serliana*, as was found in Villa Valmarana in Vigardolo and Villa Poiana. Here, however, the *serliana* is at its most abstract, with no architectural order with architraves or archivolts to define it. Bas-relief sculptures appear in rectangular niches above the rectangular openings on either side of the arch in the *serliana*. The windows in the flanking wings feature a simple cornice or frame, but no pediments.

Originally, the facade was decorated with stucco reliefs by Alessandro Vittoria, a good friend of Girolamo Forni. The original stuccos for the pediment of the villa were Winged Victories, and reliefs of the Four Seasons appeared in niches on the front and sides of the entrance loggia. Today these stuccos no longer exist; only the Medusa's head atop the arch is original. The reliefs in niches on the front of the loggia are reproductions.

Today known as the Villa Forni-Cerato, the villa is privately owned but not lived in. Its grounds can be visited by appointment.

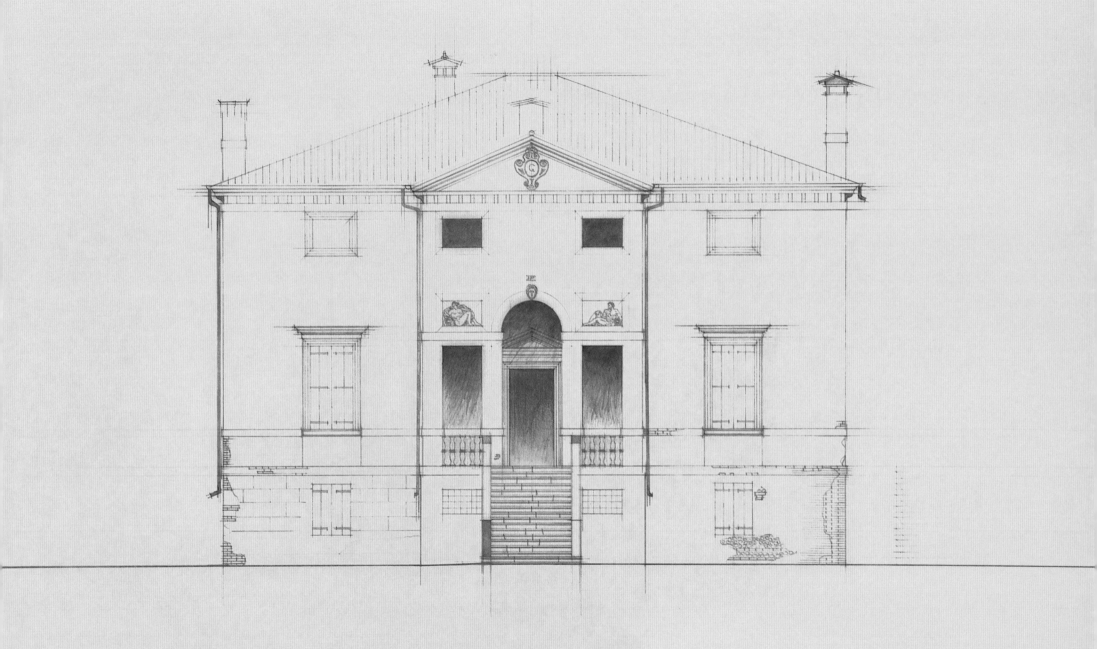

VILLA SAREGO, MIEGA
(1562/4)

As Palladio matured as an architect, his fame spread beyond Vicenza to other capitals. Thus in the late 1550s and 1560s we find a cluster of his projects in the province of Verona—one for a palace, the Palazzo della Torre in the city of Verona itself, and three villas in the surrounding countryside. His patrons for the villas were all members of the Sarego (or Serego) family, who were powerful political figures in Verona. They were also agricultural experts. Their villas had to be a combination of status symbol and functioning farm, a combination at which Palladio had come to excel.

Villa Sarego in Miega, a *frazione* of Cologna Veneta, was commissioned by Annibale Sarego in 1562. Construction began in 1564, but it was left incomplete and was subsequently almost completely destroyed. All that remains is a nine-arch arcade. Palladio provided only a brief description of the villa in the *Four Books*, with a plan and elevation of the *casa dominicale*. The plan of this villa is similar to that of Villa Badoer, where the recessed loggia opens to a long rectangular *salone* at its rear and a succession of large, medium, and small rooms on each side. The *salone* is separated from the side suites by stairwells and *studioli*.

Palladio gives no description or plan of the *barchesse*, but mentions them: "Next to this building is the courtyard for farm use, with all of the places appropriate to that function."[50] What we see today is a simplified version of the *barchesse* of the Villa Thiene at Cicogna. The arches have no frame, but imposts at the spring lines provide horizontal continuity, and the rhythm of the arcade is heightened by applied Tuscan pilasters.

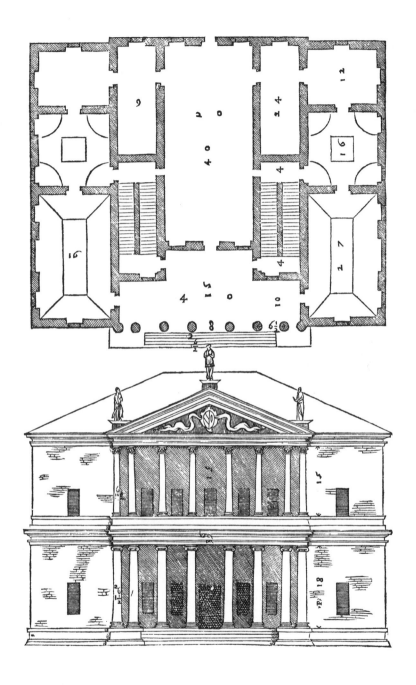

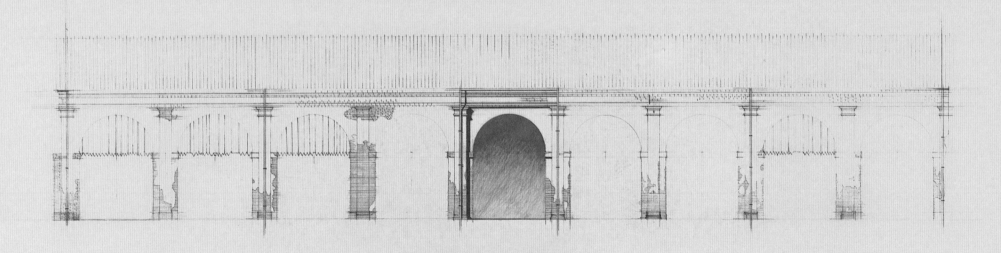

VILLA SAREGO, SANTA SOFIA
(1565–1569)

Villa Sarego in Santa Sofia, a *frazione* of Pedemonte in the province of Verona, was one of a handful of projects on which Palladio worked for different members of the Sarego (or Serego) family in the late 1560s and 1570s. It is the only one that was brought near to completion, and although today the estate itself has been greatly reduced, as much of the villa as was originally constructed remains substantially as it was in Palladio's lifetime.

Marc'Antonio Sarego was a very wealthy Veronese nobleman who was also a successful and innovative *agricoltore*, or farmer. At this time in the Veneto, the main cereals cultivated were wheat, which was consumed mainly by the wealthy and sold at a fine price, and sorghum, spelt, and millet, which produced less income. Rice was new to the Veneto, but particularly well-suited to the watery terrain. Marc'Antonio Sarego sold one of his estates so that he could invest in another on which water was plentiful in order to cultivate rice. Palladio was at first engaged by him as an engineer—not as surprising at it might seem, as his engineering skills for bridge building had been taken advantage of by Giacomo Angarano, patron of Villa Angarano, and Gianfrancesco Valmarana, patron of Villa Valmarana at Lisiera; and he had also used his skills with water management very effectively at Villa Barbaro and Villa Emo. For Marc'Antonio, Palladio installed conduits to provide and drain the water that irrigated the rice fields, and he was credited with the invention of a device to raise water.

The villa that he subsequently designed at Santa Sofia is the only surviving example of the courtyard type, which he had also used in his project for Villa Repeta. Because of its enclosed, inward-oriented nature, it is sometimes called "the villa without a facade." It is indeed the only villa by Palladio that does not have a formal entrance pavilion, nor does it have a *salone*, the single most important space in all of the other villas. What makes the villa so memorable are the colossal, rusticated Ionic columns in solemn procession around three sides of the courtyard. Villa Sarego is the only villa in which Palladio was permitted the luxury of real stone, as his columns were usually built of molded brick, which was then covered with *marmorino* to give the appearance of stone. Marc'Antonio Sarego owned the quarry from which the limestone for the columns was taken, and Palladio made the most of it, the rustication heightening the impression of solid, rough-hewn stone. In the *Four Books*, he justifies the rustication: "The columns are Ionic and made of unpolished stone, as seems appropriate here, since farms seem to require things which are rather plain and simple instead of refined."[51] The rough nature of the columns is mitigated by the fine quality of the sculptural decoration, from the Ionic capitals with their curved volutes, to the floral decoration of the frieze, to the small carved heads that decorate the cornice. Palladio was asked to create order and harmony among a group of already existing structures here, and his colossal portico served that purpose well, masking the irregularities of the existing building. Added to the rear of the columns are square pilasters, which support the weight of the second floor. A similar rusticated composite column/pilaster form was used by Palladio for a gate at the rear of Villa Pisani at Bagnolo, probably constructed some ten years before.

The U-shaped building that exists today represents about half of the project that Palladio showed in his *Four Books*. The woodcut shows a completely enclosed courtyard with the colossal colonnade on all four sides and twin staircases on one side leading up to the second-floor *piano nobile*, where symmetrical *saloni* on opposite sides were flanked by other, smaller, rooms. As we look at the villa today, we are looking at the part that corresponds to the left side of Palladio's plan. To our right would have been the hemicycle, or semicircular colonnade, and adjoining the residential courtyard to our left would have been a second, U-shaped courtyard for the farm functions. Neither the hemicycle nor the farm courtyard were ever realized.

Today the Villa Sarego-Innocenti is privately owned. The exterior may be visited by asking permission.

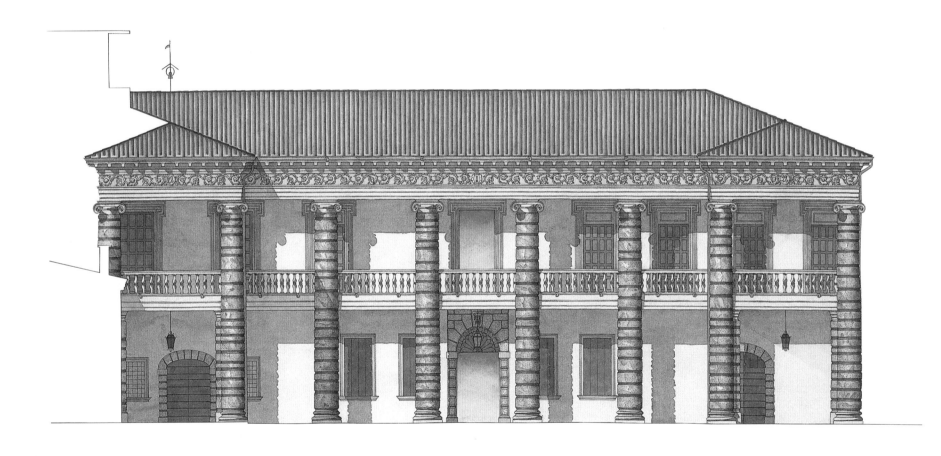

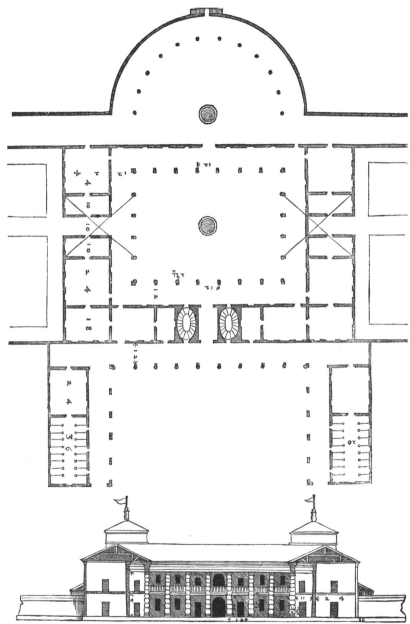

VILLA ALMERICO CAPRA, THE "ROTONDA"
(1566–1569)

Without a doubt Palladio's most famous and most influential villa is the one built at Vicenza for Paolo Almerico, best known by its nickname, the "Rotonda." The other famous building in Italian architecture that shares the same name is the Pantheon in Rome, which Palladio had studied at length and of which he provided detailed drawings in his *Four Books*. The villa's nickname is hardly modern, as the similarity between the villa and its Roman namesake had been recognized almost immediately. In 1648, English traveler John Raymond wrote that the villa took its name "from the Cupola at the top, or likeness it hath with the Pantheon in Rome."[52] That likeness was initially even more evident, as the oculus at the top of the dome was open to the sky, and rainwater was channeled through a drain in the floor to a well in the basement, exactly as in the Pantheon. The rain provided unexpected beauty, deepening the color of the terrazzo floor and reflecting, as in a mirror, the brilliant colors of the frescoes. The oculus was, for reasons easy to imagine, later closed. Its cupola, or dome, is the major feature that distinguishes the Rotonda from every other Palladian villa, and its appearance was a daring gesture on the architect's part, for until this time the dome had been associated only with religious architecture. Only partially visible as one approaches the villa, the dome crowns the cylindrical *salone* that completely dominates the interior. Passageways on the cardinal axes connect the *salone* to loggias on each of the villa's sides. The passageways also open to suites of smaller and larger rectangular rooms. The upper and lower floors are reached by interior stairs concealed in the corners of the square that surrounds the cylindrical *salone*.

The villa's commissioner, Paolo Almerico, "amongst the most respected Vicentine gentlemen,"[53] was a dignitary in the church until his retirement, when he turned to Palladio to build a suburban residence just outside the city. Because Almerico intended to use the house for pleasure and not for agriculture, Palladio hesitated to consider it a "villa" and instead included it in the section of his treatise dedicated to city houses. Nevertheless, the Rotonda has come to symbolize the quintessence of villa life. The building was designed in 1566, and although it was habitable as soon as three years later, it was still incomplete at the time of Almerico's death in 1589. In 1591 it was acquired by brothers Odorico and Marco Capra, who entrusted its completion to Palladio's invidious successor, Vicenzo Scamozzi.

Palladio's usual tripartite division of facades is evident here as well. Raised over a semibasement, the four central pavilions are given over to Ionic temple fronts, reached by stately flights of stairs. The six columns of each loggia are free standing and support an architrave and triangular pediment. The sides of the loggias open through simple arches with stylized imposts and keystones. Each architrave bears an inscription placed by the Capras. Read together, they form the phrase: MARCUS CAPRA GABRIELIS F[ILIUS]/QUI AEDES HAS ARCTISSIMO PRIMOGENITURAE GRADUI SUBJECIT/UNA CUM OMNIBUS/CENSIBUS AGRIS VALLIBUS ET COLLIBUS/CITRA VIAM MAGNAM/MEMORIAE PERPETUAE MANDANS HAEC/DUM SUSTINET AC ABSTINET ("Marco Capra son of Gabriele, who leaves this house to the closest degree of primogeniture, together with all the assets, fields, valleys and hills on our side of the great road, in eternal memory of what came to be while he sustained and abstained.") Goethe's laconic comment on this was, "This last line is very odd; a man who had so much wealth at his disposal and could do what he liked with it still feels that he ought to sustain and abstain. That lesson, surely, could have been learned at less expense."[54]

In addition to the semibasement that accommodated service spaces, and the *piano nobile* for receiving guests, the villa contained mezzanines with no windows and an upper floor for storage. The upper floor was converted to living spaces in the eighteenth century by architect Francesco Muttoni.

Palladio's design for a villa with loggias on every side was inspired by the building's splendid setting:

> The site is one of the most pleasing and delightful that one could find because it is on top of a small hill which is easy to ascend; on one side it is bathed by the Bacchiglione, a navigable river, and on the other is surrounded by other pleasant hills which resemble a vast theater and are completely cultivated and abound with wonderful fruit and excellent vines so because it enjoys the most beautiful vistas on every side, some of which are restricted, others more extensive, and yet others which end at the horizon, loggias have been built on all four sides.[55]

At last, Palladio had found the opportunity and the site that allowed him to realize an idea that he had first developed for the Villa Trissino in Meledo, some ten years earlier.

The "Rotonda" was decorated by a small army of artists, many of whom had worked with Palladio on other projects. Lorenzo Rubini, who carved the fireplaces of Villa Caldogno, executed the sculptures of the entry stairs and part of the stucco decoration in the dome and the large rectangular rooms. Other stucco decorations were undertaken by Domenico Fontana and Ruggero Bascape, who would both later work on the Teatro Olimpico. Bartolomeo Ridolfi, who worked in Villa Poiana, carved the fireplaces here. Under the patronage of the Capras, frescoes were painted by Alessandro Maganza, Palladio's companion on one of his Roman sojourns with Trissino. The statues on the acroteria of the pediments were executed in 1600 by Girolamo Albanese, who, half a century later, would create similar statues for Villa Poiana. The remaining frescoes were painted in the 1680s by the French painter Louis Dorigny.

Today the villa is the property of the Valmarana family. The *piano nobile* is open Wednesdays only for visits, while the park is open every day except Mondays.

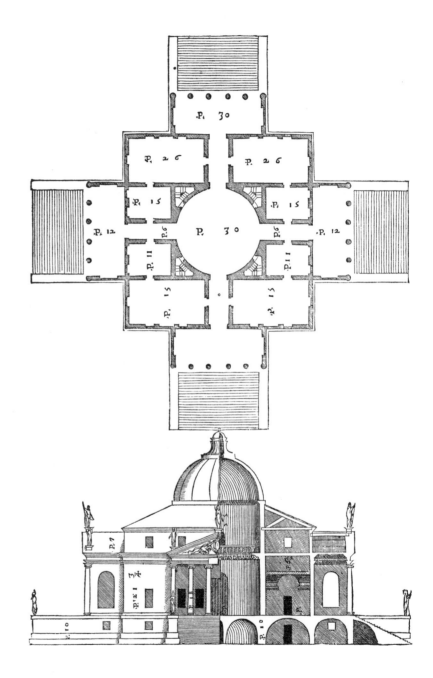

MARIVS CAPRA
GABRIELIS F

VILLA SAREGO, VERONELLA
(DATES UNKNOWN)

Villa Sarego (or Serego) at Veronella in the province of Verona, was commissioned by Federigo Sarego in 1570, but the dates of its construction are unknown. It may be due to this late date that there is no mention of this commission in the *Four Books*, which was published that year. The villa was one of four properties that Palladio was working on for members of the Sarego family. As it was to turn out, none of the villas commissioned of Palladio by the various Saregos was ever finished, perhaps because these patrons insisted that Palladio in person supervise the construction. At the time that Federigo commissioned his villa in Veronella, for instance, Palladio was busily engaged on the design of the Palazzo Barbaran in the Piazza Castello of Vicenza for Montano Barbaran. Barbaran wrote to Federigo in July 1570 saying he could not spare Palladio just then, but would send him, "as soon as I have begun work on my facade, which cannot be done without the presence of Messer Andrea Palladio."[56]

What can be seen in Veronella today is a ten-arched arcade. Similar to that designed by Palladio for the Villa Sarego at Miega, the rhythm of the succession of arches is complemented by that of the applied Tuscan pilasters. Imposts for the arches provide the only other ornamentation.

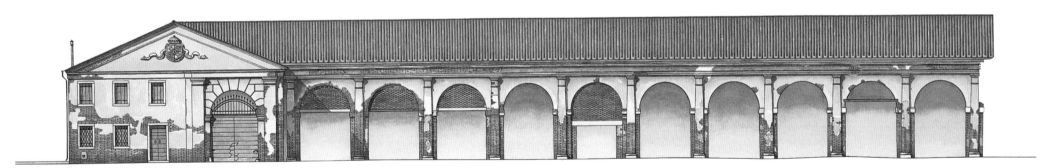

Of the last villa designed by Palladio, the Villa Porto, only the fragments of an imposing colonnade remain—a poignant testimony to both the death of the villa's patron, which brought work on the villa to a halt, and the end of the golden age of prosperity in the Veneto that gave rise to the villa phenomenon in the first place.

The columns of Villa Porto, which was commissioned by Iseppo da Porto (Iseppo is a variant of the more common Giuseppe), are located in Molina, a *frazione* of Malo, northwest of Vicenza. The Porto family was among the richest and most important in Vicenza. Iseppo married Livia Thiene, sister of Marc'Antonio and Adriano Thiene, who were also patrons of Palladio. He followed the lead of the Thiene brothers in commissioning Palladio to build first a palace as the family's city residence, then a villa as their country residence.

The ten incomplete column shafts that remain of the Villa Porto are sufficient to indicate the grandeur that was intended for the villa. The stone bases for the columns show that Palladio had planned a colonnade of the Corinthian order. Palladio may have wanted to recall the magnificence of the Pantheon in Rome, whose porch has a Corinthian colonnade, a detailed elevation of which appears in Book IV of the *Four Books*. The porch of the Pantheon has eight columns, so it is easy to imagine how imposing the colonnade of the Villa Porto with its ten columns was meant to be. Palladio gave detailed instructions about making the Corinthian order in Book I. In all the orders, the height of the column is related to the column diameter; in the case of the Corinthian, Palladio tells us that the height of the columns, including base and capital, should be nine-and-a-half times the diameter of the column. Thus, by measuring the diameter of the shafts at Villa Porto, it can be estimated that the colonnade was intended to rise to a height of nearly forty feet.

The construction of the columns of specially molded brick with curved surfaces is typical of Palladio, who reserved carved stone for the most important architectural details, such as the column bases and capitals, and the pediments of doors and windows. Once complete, the brick shafts would have been plastered with a special plastering compound known as *marmorino*. Made of lime and marble dust, when finished *marmorino* looked very much like stone. Originally developed to withstand Venice's punishing humidity, it was exceptionally long-lasting.

Here the plinths, the bottom square portion of the stone bases, are carved with the name of Iseppo Porto and the date of execution, 1572. Iseppo died in 1580, upon which construction of the villa was halted, never to resume. Palladio also died in 1580. This unfinished work is a memorial to both patron and architect.

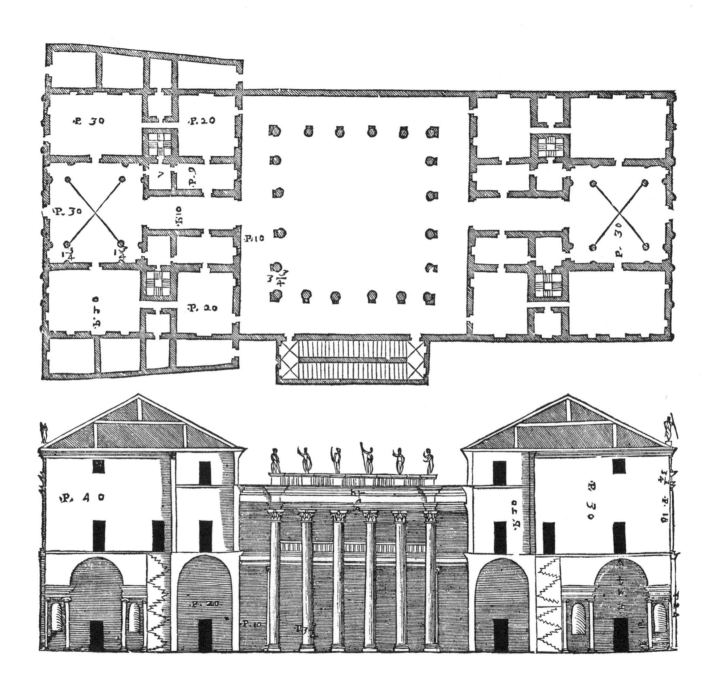

VILLA PORTO A MOLINA DI MALO

VILLA CONTARINI
(1547, 1676–1684)

Villa Contarini is traditionally attributed to Palladio, but is so altered today that the original Palladian contributions can hardly be discerned. Brothers Francesco and Paolo Contarini commissioned Palladio to build a villa on their land in Piazzola sul Brenta, in the province of Padua, in 1547. The Contarini family was legendary for their wealth, and they were very powerful politically. Eight Venetian doges and forty-eight *procuratori* were members of the Contarini family.

Little is left of Palladio's original design except for the three-part division of the villa's main block and the two *serliana* that flank the main entrance. The present Baroque appearance of the villa is a result of several remodeling campaigns from the seventeenth century on. In 1676, the wings and columned porticoes that define the immense courtyard in front of the villa (the *barchesse*, which by now no longer had anything to do with farm work) were added. The side wings have rusticated columns and colossal statues of men, known as telamons, supporting the cornices. The frescoes inside were painted in 1684, mainly by Michele Primon.

Villa Contarini provides an excellent opportunity to see how the concept of the villa changed in the decades after Palladio's time. In the mid-seventeenth century, Villa Contarini became the property of Marco Contarini, who was the *procuratore* of San Marco, a prestigious title given to the overseer of the Basilica of San Marco. By this time, the villa had lost its connotation as a functioning farm and was seen as a noble residence in the countryside. In keeping with this and with his position as one of the highest dignitaries of Venice, Count Contarini transformed his villa into a Baroque palace. The villa was also provided with the amenities necessary for entertainment: not just one but two theaters, a concert hall, a music school for children, pleasure gardens in which to stroll. In its time, the entertainment at Villa Contarini could not be excelled. In 1685, Count Contarini received the Duke of Braunschweig for a three-day state visit. The villa's beautiful courtyard provided a suitable backdrop for the arrival of the duke, which was the occasion for non-stop festivities, including spectacles on land and on the Brenta River, such as the reevocation of a naval battle between two Venetian warships against a Turkish galleon, and theatre performances with as many as five hundred actors.

Today the Villa Contarini-Camerini is privately owned by a pharmaceutical company that meticulously restored it and transformed it into a museum. It is open for visits. The courtyard in front of the villa is state-owned.

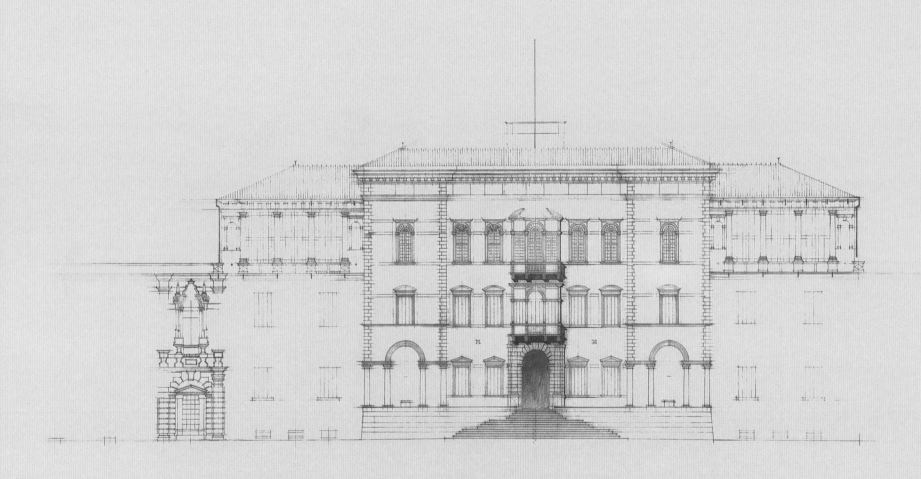

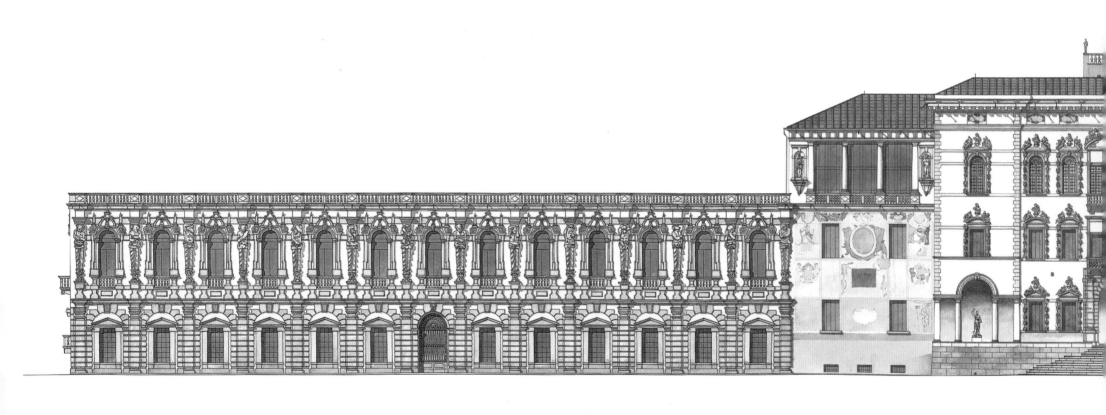

VILLA PORTO, VIVARO
(1550s, 1855)

Villa Porto is located in Vivaro, a *frazione* of Dueville ("two villas"), off of the provincial road between Vicenza and Bassano del Grappa. Count Paolo Porto was a member of Vicenza's distinguished Porto family and a relative of Iseppo Porto, who had commissioned Palladio to build the Palazzo Porto in Vicenza and the Villa Porto in Molina di Malo. Paolo inherited the land from his father in 1554, and although the villa does not appear in the *Four Books*, it is traditionally attributed to Palladio. In terms of its architectural style, it is easy to understand the attribution. The villa's facade shows the tripartite division of symmetrical side blocks flanking a central loggia. The loggia is articulated by a colossal Ionic temple front, whose pediment is adorned with the family crest. Statues are arranged classically on the corners of the villa, on its pediment, and at the base of the stairs leading up to the loggia.

If Palladio was indeed involved, it is likely that he was only responsible for the nucleus of the villa, and that it was completed under the direction of another architect in the late 1580s, after Palladio's death. What is certain is that it was given its actual, Palladian, form in 1855 by architect Antonio Caregaro Negrin. Caregaro Negrin relied heavily on Palladio's illustrations in the *Four Books*. The flanking wings of the villa, which has a semibasement, *piano nobile*, and upper floor, were modeled on Palladio's illustration in the *Four Books* for the Villa Pisani in Montagnana.

Today known as the Villa da Porto del Conte and privately owned, the villa can be seen from miles around rising majestically over the plain. While the exterior of the villa is always visible, its interior is usually closed.

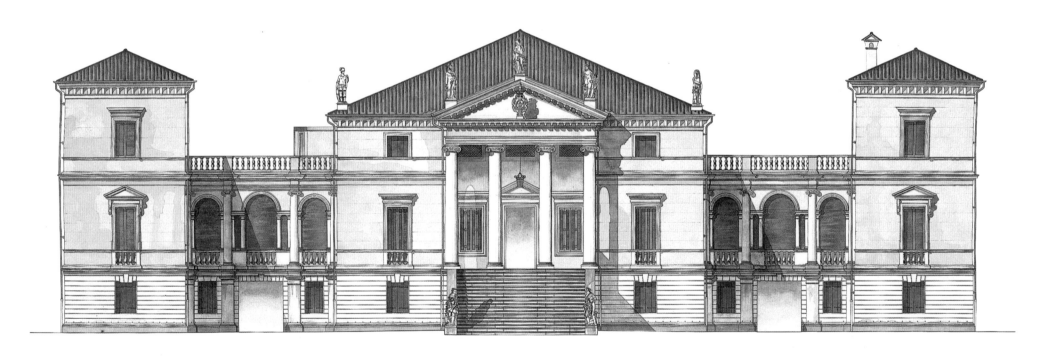

145

NOTES

I would like to dedicate the text for this book to Carl and Sally Gable, owners of the Villa Cornaro.

1. In the *Four Books* the elevations of Villa Cornaro at Piombino Dese and the Villa Pisani at Montagnana are actually quite similar, but the plans show clearly that only Villa Cornaro has a projecting central loggia, while that of Villa Pisani is merely applied to the surface. See pp. 68 and 72.
2. Palladio's drawings are now mainly in the collections of the Royal Institute of British Architects (RIBA) and the Museo Civico in Vicenza.
3. Andrea Palladio, *The Four Books of Architecture*, trans. Robert Tavernor and Richard Schofield (Cambridge, MA: MIT Press, 1997), viii.
4. Quoted in Bruce Boucher, *Andrea Palladio: The Architect in His Time* (New York: Abbeville Press, 1994), 26 and 306, note 47.
5. Palladio, *The Four Books*, 3.
6. Palladio, *The Four Books*, 5.
7. Giorgio Vasari, *Le vite dei più eccellenti pittori, scultori e architetti* (Rome: Newton Compton, 1991), 1315.
8. Johann Wolfgang von Goethe, *Italian Journey*, trans. W. H. Auden and Elizabeth Mayer (London: Penguin Books, 1970), 103.
9. Goethe, *Italian Journey*, 70.
10. Quoted in William Howard Adams, ed., *The Eye of Jefferson* (Washington D.C.: National Gallery of Art, 1976), 283. I am grateful to Rachel Fletcher for this reference.
11. Vasari, *Le vite*, 1315.
12. Because Palladio was so precise in the use of these elements and so deliberate, in the sense that his ornament is never superficial but performs a function—such as when the architrave at Villa Pisani at Montagnana is carried all the way around the villa as a unifying device—it is necessary to use precise terminology to describe it. To this end, a short glossary accompanies the text and explains specific architectural terms. Included are definitions of some of Palladio's favorite motifs (colossal orders, pediments, thermal windows, specific types of roofs and vaults, etc.) as well as some Italian terms that appear frequently.
13. James S. Ackerman, *Palladio's Villas* (Locust Valley, NY: J. J. Augustin Publisher, 1990), 89.
14. Palladio, *The Four Books*, 121.
15. Palladio, *The Four Books*, 123.
16. Palladio, *The Four Books*, 135.
17. The dates cited in the text refer usually to the period of construction. In some cases where documentation is scarce, dates are approximated based on stylistic considerations; in other cases, the date for the commission may be known but not the dates for construction. When more than one time period is given, this indicates successive building phases.
18. Palladio, *The Four Books*, 143.
19. Palladio, *The Four Books*, 143.
20. Palladio, *The Four Books*, 17 and 61.

21. RIBA XVII/2r.

22. RIBA XVII/19.

23. RIBA XVII/2r.

24. RIBA XVII/27.

25. Palladio, *The Four Books*, 124.

26. Vasari, *Le vite*, 1314.

27. Worcester College Library, Oxford, England (Archive number H.T. 89).

28. Palladio, *The Four Books*, 134.

29. RIBA XVII, 20av.

30. Palladio, *The Four Books*, 136.

31. RIBA XVII/2r.

32. Palladio, *The Four Books*, 141.

33. Palladio, *The Four Books*, 17.

34. Palladio, *The Four Books*, 123.

35. Museo Civico, Vicenza (Archive number D26).

36. Palladio, *The Four Books*, 17.

37. RIBA XVI, 20A r.

38. Palladio, *The Four Books*, 17 and 61.

39. Palladio, *The Four Books*, 67.

40. Palladio, *The Four Books*, 129.

41. Palladio, *The Four Books*, 129.

42. Palladio, *The Four Books*, 165.

43. Vasari, *Le vite*, 1314.

44. Palladio, *The Four Books*, 139.

45. Palladio, *The Four Books*, 138.

46. RIBA IX/7.

47. Palladio, *The Four Books*, 20.

48. Palladio, *The Four Books*, 127.

49. Vasari, *Le vite*, 1314.

50. Palladio, *The Four Books*, 146.

51. Palladio, *The Four Books*, 144.

52. John Raymond, *An Itinerary Contayning a Voyage Made Through Italy* (London: np, 1648), 225.

53. Palladio, *The Four Books*, 94.

54. Goethe, *Italian Journey*, 67.

55. Palladio, *The Four Books*, 94.

56. Gian Giorgio Zorzi, *Le ville e I teatri di Andrea Palladio* (Venice: Neri Pozza, 1965), 257; quoted in Bruce Boucher, *Andrea Palladio: The Architect in His Time* (New York: Abbeville Press, 1994), 279.

ACROTERION (pl. acroteria). A pedestal or platform supporting a statue or ornament on the corners of a building or at the ends and peak of a pediment.

ARCHITECTURAL ORDER. A given style of column and the elaborated horizontal members (the entablature) carried by it. Palladio describes five orders in the *Four Books* (Tuscan, Doric, Ionic, Corinthian, and Composite).

ARCHITRAVE. The lowest horizontal member of the entablature, resting upon the column capitals.

ARCHIVOLT. An architrave in the form of an arch.

BARCHESSA (pl. *barchesse*). The agricultural wings of a villa, providing storage and workrooms, as well as a covered corridor so that the villa's owner is protected from the elements as he supervises the work on his property.

BROKEN PEDIMENT. A triangular pediment in which either the apex or the base is split apart. Palladio eschewed the pediment broken at its apex as structurally unstable, but a pediment with a broken base appears at Villa Foscari and Villa Poiana.

CASA DOMINICALE. The patron's or owner's house in a villa complex; the main residential block.

COLOSSAL ORDER. An architectural order that encompasses more than one story.

COLUMNS *IN ANTIS*. A colonnade in which the two outermost columns are connected (engaged) to end walls; literally "between pilasters."

CORNICE. The uppermost horizontal element in the entablature of an order; the horizontal frame crowning a door or window.

DENTILS. Small rectangular blocks that are part of the entablatures of the Ionic, Corinthian, and Composite orders; intended to represent the ends of beams or rafters; literally "teeth."

FRAZIONE. An outlying village that is governed by a larger municipality in the near vicinity.

FRIEZE. The horizontal band between the architrave and the cornice, usually carved with animals, flowers, or human figures.

HEMICYCLE. A colonnade in the form of a semicircle; other semicircular forms such as stairways.

IN ANTIS. See COLUMNS *IN ANTIS*.

INTONACO. The finished plaster coat applied to the interior and exterior of masonry walls.

LOGGIA. A short colonnade on the front of a house or temple, which can be either recessed or projecting; a porch.

MARMORINO. A plasterlike compound made from several layers of lime and marble dust. It could be easily colored by the addition of minerals, and was long-lasting and humidity-resistant. The marble dust in the mixture and a particular surface treatment rendered it very like marble in appearance. It was frequently used for wall surfaces and to cover the bricks of which Palladio constructed his columns.

METOPES. Panels in the Doric frieze that alternate with triglyphs to form a running decoration. Metopes are often carved. In the Villa Pisani at Montagnana the metopes are decorated with a *bucranium*, a sculptured ornament featuring the head of an ox.

OCULUS (pl. oculi). A round opening, either in a wall or a vault.

PEDIMENT. The triangular gabled end of a roof, often bearing the family coat of arms.

PIANO NOBILE (pl. *piani nobili*). The main residential floor of the patron's house with formal reception rooms, or *saloni*, usually raised above a full or semibasement and reached by the stairs.

PILASTER. A pier or column that is applied to the wall rather than free-standing.

PORTICO. A long colonnade used for courtyards and agricultural wings (*barchesse*); the colonnade of a portico is longer than that of a loggia.

PRONAOS. In classical architecture, the columned space in front of the inner cell of a temple, upon which Palladio based his loggia.

PROVINCE (*provincia*). An area of local government, similar to a county in the United States, having its center in the *capoluogo*, or county seat.

QUOINS. Stones or bricks used to reinforce corners or edges of walls, sometimes imitated in plaster for aesthetic effect.

RAKING CORNICE. The slanting cornice that forms the upper edge of a triangular pediment.

RUSTICATION. Stone facing featuring deeply cut joints and rough-textured faces used to create an impression of solidity and impregnability; may be imitated in plaster.

SALONE. The main hall for receiving guests and entertainment, usually in the center of the *piano nobile* of a villa.

SERLIANA. A type of tripartite window or door with a central arched opening flanked by two lower rectangular openings. Originally named after Sebastiano Serlio, now also known as a Palladian window or door.

SPRING LINE. The horizontal line at which an arch or vault begins its curve.

STRING MOLDING. A continuous, projecting molding that extends across the surface of a facade and may also cross vertical features such as pilasters, columns, window frames, etc. May be simple or elaborate.

TELAMON. A sculpture in the form of a man used in place of a column to support an architrave; sometimes called an *atlas*.

TERRAFERMA. The land holdings of the Venetians; literally "solid ground."

THERMAL WINDOW. A semicircular window divided into three vertical parts. So called because it was first used in the Roman *thermae*, or baths.

TRIGLYPHS. An ornamental panel of the Doric frieze consisting of three vertical bands, which may or may not be fluted, separated by grooves. Triglyphs alternate with metopes on the frieze.

TRIPARTITE. Divided into three parts.

TYMPANUM. The triangular surface of a pediment, sometimes ornamented with sculpture or low relief. Palladio often placed the family coat of arms in the tympanum.

VAULT. A masonry covering or ceiling over a space based upon construction of the arch. Palladio described six kinds of vaults in the *Four Books*: round vaults on either a circular base or on spandrels, cross vaults, segmental vaults, cove vaults, lunette vaults, barrel vaults.

VENETAN. Of the Veneto region.

VICENTINE. Of the city of Vicenza.

VILLA. A country estate or farm consisting of the patron's house (*casa dominicale*) and agricultural wings (*barchesse*), plus forecourts, ornamental gardens, vegetable gardens, orchards, fishponds, and agricultural fields. More commonly the term *villa* refers only to the patron's house.

VOUSSOIRS. Wedge-shaped stones that form an arch. The central voussoir is the "keystone."

Ackerman, James S. *Palladio's Villas*. Locust Valley, NY: J. J. Augustin Publisher, 1967.

___. *The Villa*. Princeton, NJ: Princeton University Press, 1990.

___. *Palladio*. London: Penguin Books, 1991.

Andrea Palladio—Il Veneto (CD-ROM). Vicenza: Regione Veneto Istituto per le Ville Venete and Centro Internazionale di Studi di Architettura Andrea Palladio, 1990.

Bertotti-Scamozzi, Ottavio. *Le fabbriche e i disegni di Andrea Palladio*. 4 vols. 1776–1783. Reprint, Trento: La Roccia, 1976.

Bödefeld, Gerda and Berthold Hinz. *Ville Venete*. Milan: Idealibri, 1990.

Boucher, Bruce. *Andrea Palladio: The Architect in His Time*. New York: Abbeville Press, 1994.

Constant, Caroline. *The Palladio Guide*. 2nd ed. New York: Princeton Architectural Press, 1993.

Goethe, Johann Wolfgang von. *Italian Journey*. W. H. Auden and Elizabeth Mayer, trans. London: Penguin Books, 1970.

Gualdo, Paolo. "La vita di Andrea Palladio." Ed. Gian Giorgio Zorzi. In *Saggi e memorie di storia dell'arte* 2 (1958–59), 91–104.

Holberton, Paul. *Palladio's Villa: Life in the Renaissance Countryside*. London: John Murray, 1990.

Kimball, S. Fiske. *Thomas Jefferson, Architect*. (1916) Reprint. New York: Da Capo, 1968.

Palladio, Andrea. *The Four Books of Architecture*. Robert Tavernor and Richard Schofield, trans. Cambridge, MA: MIT Press, 1997.

Puppi, Lionello. *Andrea Palladio: Opera completa*. Milan: Electa, 1986.

Raymond, John. *An Itinerary Contayning a Voyage Made Through Italy*. London, 1648.

Tavernor, Robert. *Palladio and Palladianism*. London: Thames and Hudson, 1991.

Vasari, Giorgio. *Le vite dei più eccellenti pittori, scultori e architetti*. Rome: Newton Compton, 1991.

Wittkower, Rudolf. *Architectural Principles in the Age of Humanism*. New York: W. W. Norton, 1971.

Wundram Manfred, Thomas Pape, and Paolo Marton. *Andrea Palladio*. Cologne: Benedikt Taschen Verlag, 1999.

Zorzi, Gian Giorgio. *Le ville e i teatri di Andrea Palladio*. Venice: Neri Pozza, 1968.